Training   Coaching   Development

THE
SOCIAL
COMPASS

Time Tested Methods to
Communicate Better, Understand
Others, Resolve Conflict & Keep Your Project
& Team at the Top

GWYNNE N. DAWDY, Ph.D.

Wasteland Press
Shelbyville, KY USA
www.wastelandpress.net

The Social Compass:
Time Tested Methods to Communicate Better,
Understand Others, Resolve Conflict & Keep Your
Project & Team at the Top
by Gwynne N. Dawdy, Ph.D.

First Printing – August 2006
ISBN13: 978-1-60047-039-4
ISBN 10: 1-60047-039-4

Printed In U.S.A.

In loving memory of my gram: Mary Jungewaelter, my granny: Dee Dawdy, my uncles: Louie and Al, and my dear companion: Zaphroid.

I miss you.

Contents

Chapter Eight

"Need direction? Where do I turn next? What a great book! Highly motivating and results oriented. Lots of practical knowledge of behavior and communication styles guaranteed to unlock potential and talent. A useful book for those who care about success in today's working environment. True stories, effective axioms and powerful concepts."

Deborah J. Bauman, M. Ed., *InMotion*

Prelude

Behavioral, social, and communication styles are the most common topics in my coaching conversations and workshops. Project managers and leaders seek a cohesive, cooperative, and results-oriented team. It seems like a simple vision, but it tends to be one of great struggle. Why? People are unique. We are the one variable in the equation that does not remain constant. Personalities clash, social styles vary, people behave differently and communication preferences adjust across the board. Needless to say, these matters make for interesting projects and team management. These people-issues are the core of this book.

From years of training professionals, the demand for understanding others continues to escalate. I have frequently been asked: "Dr. Dawdy, how do I influence people of all levels within my project?" "How does a project manager or team leader effectively lead, manage and follow a group of supervisors, peers, and customers?" "How can I communicate the importance of tasks to subordinates when some people can not see the big picture?" "What are the most common people-oriented problems within projects and what can I do as a Project Manager to avoid or mitigate those problems?" The goal of this writing is to answer these questions (and more) and empower project managers and team leaders so that they may empower their team.

The purpose of The Social Compass is four-fold. First, this book will investigate the dynamics of human behavior and communication preferences so project managers and leaders can better influence those with whom they work. Second, we will examine the most effective means to communicate for enhanced results with less human effort. Third, we shall identify the most common problems in the workplace, particularly those related to social styles, projects, and team management. Last, we will explore and answer project managers' most frequently asked questions regarding these issues, as well as the issues of improving performance and success.

People often ask, "Why does she/he act this way?" Not only is that a question of underlying motivation, but it is also a pressing question of behavioral pattern. As in many fields, in order to predict future trends, one must look at past mile markers. This is no different for predicting personal behavior. Recognizing preferred patterns may aid in understanding future behavior. However, this also means that people may act differently in different situations. So, keep in mind the need to recognize this variation of degree in behavior.

By understanding the different degrees of social style, one can apply various techniques which aid in project design, management or results. When I mention behavioral and communication styles, typically I receive a groan and the comment, "you can't box me into a label." True. This is the reason behind the Compass term. People are dynamic. We are not one-sided. Chapter One offers a more detailed exploration of the Social Compass terminology and logic.

From there, each prominent social style is explored in Chapter Two. These four preferences include the Navigator, the Explorer, the Social Servitor, and the Worker. The social styles are based on a wide research of behavioral and communication styles. While each has unique qualities, the theoretical foundation of dispositional characteristics remains constant. This text and the Social Compass profile are not personality assessments. Rather, this book is meant to explore how people typically react to different situations. Studies have noted that individuals may each react to the same situation in a way different from other people. It is the purpose of the Social Compass to gain a greater understanding of an individual's typical behavioral response and how that response can be enhanced based on their preferred style.

Furthering the exploration of social styles in the workplace, Chapter Three explores the strengths and Chapter Four delves into the stressors for each style. It is not sufficient to strengthen the strengths. To truly excel, people must also address their stressors. It is important to recognize this for yourself and your team members. It may aid in proper job placement, recognition, training, development and interaction.

Once these social preferences are understood, it is important to recognize the dominant style of your team members, C-level players, or customers. Chapter Five explores tips and tools to accurately identify an individual's dominant communication method.

Knowing how to identify one's preferred style, strengths and stressors is not enough. Successful negotiation, communication, influence, and performance enhancement require behavioral adaptation. This may take practice, but once mastered, it is a tool that leads to tremendous success. Methods for this mastery are discussed in Chapter Six.

No matter how hard we work at building a strong team and project, there are always problems. These problems may be predictable, or may be surprises. Project managers tend to be fantastic at predicting, taking, and managing risk. However, team members may not be as prepared. In this, it is inevitable that problems arise within a team. Many of these problems are social issues. For instance, it is estimated that over 30% of a project manager's time is spent troubleshooting issues relating to poor communication. Chapter Seven explores issues like this and discusses ways to deal with people and workplace problems.

After surveying project managers across the country, I have collected the most pressing questions posed. Many of them relate to communication and behavior of those on their team. These individuals include supervisors, customers, stakeholders and team members. I have devised some strategies that project managers and team leaders may find useful. Chapter Eight visits these strategies.

The final chapters summarize this text, discuss the research involved and explore my services and credentials.

I hope you find this writing to be reader friendly and full of immediately useful tools. It is my goal to add to your management repertoire so that you are empowered and can raise the results of your team.

Chapter One
The Social Compass

There have been a number of studies and research on personality styles, social preferences and behavior. Many organizations use profiles like the Myers-Briggs Type Indicator (MBTI) in their battery of tests for new employees. These types of assessments are also incorporated into training for leadership development, team cohesion, management styles and enhanced communication. This is the primary use of profiles in my company: to enhance relations and performance within a team, department, or family.

Project managers and team leaders find this type of training to be extremely effective. By recognizing prominent communication and action preferences, pesky and time consuming issues stemming from miscommunication may be prevented.

The greatest question that seems to be posed within many fields is: why do people act the way they do? While there are no sound means to 100% accurately define someone's future actions, there are a number of tools that work together to predict how one may act or react in a given situation. This is important to know in the work place, where human behavior can be the deciding factor between success and failure.

Companies, organizations, athletic teams and other groups have been interested in how members will receive one another. Will there be strong cohesion? Will there be great strife? Will everyone try to lead and be competitive with one another? Will no one step up to the leadership position and will everyone prefer to follow? Will people be afraid to take risks? Will others take too many risks without connection to consequences or regulations? The list of questions related to behavioral styles and thought process goes on and on. In order to answer these questions as best we can, behavioral profiles, leadership assessments, and team instruments are implemented.

While there are many benefits to these profiles, clients have often addressed their concerns of being labeled and of the accuracy of these assessments. These are great concerns! Some profiles offer categories as if individuals are clearly one type or the other, with little ability to adjust. Some profiles strictly assess personality styles, which typically remain constant over time and are very difficult to change. Some profiles may consider different types to be like a map or a line on which people fall with regards to their social and communication style. I agree to the extent that we are a complex sum of personalities, experiences and situations. In this, individuals may consist of one dominant behavioral or communication style, with another preference running a quick second. I also believe that people will adjust their styles to maintain a healthy equilibrium. Perhaps we act differently at home than we do at work. Perhaps we act differently at work with cohorts than we do with supervisors or subordinates. Perhaps we act differently with one team project than with another team project. In this, the social compass does not address or assess your core personality. It does address your typical reaction, thought process and communication preference in a given situation.

One of the first people to address this issue was Walter Mischel. In 1968, he proposed that our behaviors are not merely defined by one's personality. He suggested that how people perceive their situation also has a profound impact in how they react or behave. This is such an important concept. When people take profiles, the most common response I hear is, "how do I take this? I act differently at home than at work!" This is a great insight for us to have. Mischel took this observation and developed the "formula" by which we can more accurately measure one's typical behavioral style. The simple principle is this: Behavior = Personality x Perception/Interpretation of the Situation.

It is this reason that I have used the concept of the compass in exploring human behavior. For instance, you may exhibit Navigator qualities when at work with a team project, keeping the big picture in focus and managing various members within the project. Once that issue or meeting has adjourned, you may need to adjust direction and connect with customers to summarize the team meeting. You may need to go over every detail discussed and verify any step-by-step changes which may have been made. In this, you need to sway towards the Worker style. After that appointment, you may need to go to your child's basketball game and reconnect with other parents and community members. This situation may call for a change in social direction towards the Social Servitor style. At home, when everyone has relaxed and is enjoying the evening, you may find the space to think, to brainstorm issues that may be influencing your project, to creatively try new ideas or consider innovative resolutions. This may sway your style in the direction of the Explorer. All in a day's work!

Most people will continue through these events, highly influenced by their dominant style. What does this mean? Well, even in a social setting like a child's basketball game, someone whose preferred style is that of the Navigator may discuss things in concepts of big-picture, accomplishment, competition, and goals. In this same setting, a Social Servitor may discuss things in concepts of team connection, personal stories, reflection, and development. A Worker may discuss things in detail, in brief context and in a more reserved manner. An Explorer may discuss things in terms of adventure and newness, with great energy, and in a more outgoing manner. While the setting of the basketball game has encouraged the conversational style to be more social, the preferred, dominant manner shines through in the communication discourse.

The Mariner's Compass

So, let us look at the compass tool in more detail. Originally devised by Chinese mariners, it was meant to help find directions on the earth more easily and accurately than the previous method of celestial navigation. It has four main points for direction: north, south, east, and west. The needle sways as directions are altered, pointing towards the earth's magnetic field. By using this compass, travelers know their direction and heading.

Many compasses also include degree markers between the cardinal points of north, south, east, and west. Why is this important? A caravan may be heading due east across the entire United States. However, if they adjust heading by even one degree, they may find themselves miles and miles off their targeted arrival location. To correct this error, many mariners also use other instruments like the clock and the sextant to provide accurate navigation.

Why have we spent time reviewing the history of the compass? Because the navigational tool used to direct people towards a particular goal is paralleled in this book to a social tool used to direct towards a particular behavioral goal.

Now that we have explored the basics of the mariner's compass, we can further identify how the social tool can direct us to a greater understanding of human behavior. It may be used to reach the goals of higher performance, enhanced communication, better relations, and more effective project and team management.

The Social Compass

The mariner's tool is used to guide people to reach their intended destination. It does not formulate the goals, but it does direct people to stay on target so they may reach their objectives more easily. The Social Compass is much the same. It does not create the communication goals, but it does serve as a tool for greater understanding and more effective communication. By recognizing the four cardinal styles (Navigator, Social Servitor, Explorer and Worker), as well as the degree markers for adjustment between these cardinal points, individuals can navigate their way towards greater performance.

How does this work? First, there must be a goal (destination) in mind. For instance, one may need to facilitate a meeting to discuss project changes. This meeting may be with the engineers and members who need to know the tiniest details and the step by step direction of change. In this, one's goal may be to disseminate the information as efficiently and as accurately as possible. To do this, the individual would need to recognize the preferred style of the members of the group. This is where the Social Compass comes into play. The Social Compass would then direct the individual towards the preferred cardinal direction. Navigation towards that communication style is smooth, and the goal (efficiently and accurately sharing information) is met.

What happens without the Social Compass? Typically, a manager will enter a group with the knowledge of facts and information to share. Often, the focus is on the message, and not on the delivery. When this is the case, the manager will speak in a manner comfortable and familiar to him. If the members of the group do not share the same communication preference as the manager, they may tune out, may misunderstand the information, may become frustrated with the delivery of the message, or may end up with more questions than answers. From this, individuals seek one-on-one time to clarify the information.

People may also ignore what was offered, out of frustration and confusion. This leads to ineffective performance. This also leads to a waste of time in following up with these individuals to fix the issues from ineffective communication. The intention was good, but this type of process and delivery can actually prevent efficient and effective communication.

> *Drawing on my fine command of language, I said nothing* ~ Robert Charles Benchley

Many of you may have been in this situation before. Some of you identify with the frustrated listener. Others may identify with the theme-focused facilitator. The rest may identify with both parties, having led meetings and been in meetings that end in communication disarray.

The good news is that leading teams and managing projects do not have to be this way. We don't have to look at the stars for answers. We now have tools like the Social Compass to guide us to more effective, efficient, and accurate information. This, in turn, leads to greater morale, higher performance, and an enhanced sense of self and teamwork.

The Cardinal Points on the Social Compass

Recall that people are not one-dimensional. We fluctuate as needed. We have depth stemming from unique experiences, education, beliefs, and perceptions. However, most of the time our conversational and behavioral manners are influenced by our most preferred social style (and the great majority of folks who have taken behavioral, communication, or personality assessments comment that they feel they do have a most-preferred style). The most successful leaders are those who can adjust their communication styles to match the preferred styles of others. In this, communication is received more efficiently, accurately and even more openly.

The Navigator

The Navigator is the dispositional style most associated with leadership. This social manner involves influence, competition, goals, big vision, and accomplishment. Often, those who have a greater Navigator preference are driven towards success. They invite challenge, encourage competition, and strive towards great heights. These people may be more assertive in offering opinion, and may often be construed as aggressive with a know-it-all attitude.

This social style is termed the Navigator for several reasons. I wanted to follow the N, S, E, W points on the compass. The Navigator term was chosen because people with this preference are born leaders and visionaries. Often, other types will naturally gravitate towards Navigators for answers, for direction, and for leadership. Many find the Navigator to be a magnetic personality, drawing others toward them (even with their assertive or aggressive tones) much like the compass will point towards the north because of the earth's magnetic field.

Additionally, Navigators tend to be the types to easily see the big picture while attending to the more important details. They confidently face challenges and changes, and can steer or navigate their team through many storms without outwardly panicking.

The Social Servitor

The Social Servitor is the dispositional style most associated with social people. This manner involves teamwork, cooperation, talking, connection, empathy, and personal growth. Often, those who have a greater Social Servitor preference are driven towards connecting with others. They invite open conversations, warm relations, friendly atmospheres and philosophical discussions. These people may be more interested in sharing personal experiences and feelings than in assertive opinions. They may be construed as those who will do just about anything for anyone out of the goodness of their hearts.

This social style is termed the Social Servitor for a couple of reasons. Again, I wanted to stay with the compass points N, S, E, W. Additionally, the Social Servitor term was chosen because people with this dispositional preference are born servers with social dynamics. Often, they feel a sense of belonging and purpose when they can be of service to others. Not only that, they thrive in social settings where conversation can lead to team cohesion. In this, they may seem to be direct opposites of the Navigator types.

Furthermore, Social Servitors are interested in the effects a decision will have on the group and individuals. They can see both the big picture and the details when pressed, but prefer to focus on the impact these decisions will have on each member. Thus, they are democratic by nature.

In the midst of storms, they are fantastic at working with others to enhance comfort levels. They do not typically navigate or give orders, but they do listen and mediate well between different parties, thus the term Social Servitor.

The Explorer

The Explorer is the dispositional style most associated with the adventurous spirit. This social manner involves creativity, adventure, innovation, exploration, newness, and vision. Often, those who have an Explorer preference are driven towards independence. They invite challenge, desire autonomy, and embrace change. They often despise regulations, especially if those regulations restrict the ability for creative expression and freedom.

This term was chosen for this disposition because people with this preference are born explorers. They thrive to discover new things, to be the master of their domain, to throw away the clock and rules in the name of creativity. Often, other types may think the Explorers to be rebellious, flighty, or eccentric. However, these very traits are what make the Explorer types unique.

If we did not have the Explorer, many things would be different. It is because of this type and their nature that we live in our great land, that we have the inventions we know today, and that we enjoy various freedoms that we may take for granted. Without this preferred disposition, change is not sought. The world would not be anywhere near as advanced or as artistically colorful.

In addition, this type has a natural tendency for optimism. This may be the driving force that keeps them creative. When one idea fails, they are optimistic that the next will work. After criticizing his "failures" while inventing the light bulb, Thomas Edison replied "I did not fail. I found 10,000 ways that did not work." This is the nature of the Explorer.

The Worker

The Worker is the dispositional style most associated with the diligent and dedicated individual. This social manner involves a tremendous attention to detail. This disposition also encourages diligence, reliability, and stability. Often, those who have a Worker preference are driven towards complete structure and project perfection. They invite logic and offer reserved but analytical discussion.

This term was chosen for this type because people of this preference are born workers. They thrive to complete tasks, and complete them right. They live by the rules and honor intricacies. Others may think this type to be rigid and inflexible. However, these very traits are what have brought many creative ideas and inventions to life.

Like the Navigator, this type is very focused on goal attainment. Unlike the Navigator, the Worker prides on perfection more than time, so may need to be occasionally reminded of deadlines. Unlike the Navigator, he Worker is much more reserved and quietly attends to the task at hand.

As you may have guessed, the Worker and Explorer seem to be opposites. Yet, both compliment one another tremendously. Many times, this pair may work well together if their strengths and tendencies are honored. For instance, when an Explorer is allowed to brainstorm and creatively invent a new product, and a Worker is allowed to structure the details of the product's fruition, the team can work wonders. Some liken the Explorer to be the architect and the Worker to be the builder. Neither can succeed without the other. Both have to understand the process of the other's work in order to excel on their end.

Throughout this book, it is my hope that you will see that we do vary among these four preferences. There is no right or wrong preference, and neither behavioral or communication style is better than the other. They are simply different, and those differences are important to recognize and even adapt in order to communicate more accurately. The most successful individuals are able to adjust their conversational and behavioral style to match the style of others. In this, they are able to get more from others with less effort.

The following chapters will discuss these qualities in greater detail. We will address the most common questions asked of me by project managers and team leaders. With this, you will have a greater understanding of human nature and may be able to better your project and team.

"The rung of a ladder was never meant to rest upon, but only to support your weight long enough so you can reach for something higher." ~ Anonymous

Chapter Two
The Preferred Styles

"Why does Suzie say that? How is it that John can work all of these numbers and stick to the rules? Jozie just wants to change things for the sake of change, is she nuts? Denny is so bossy, I can't believe he has gotten where he is without any people-skills."

Do these scenarios and questions sound familiar? Often, conflict and misunderstandings occur because people do not appreciate the different strengths others may bring to the table. We know what we understand. When we don't understand each other, we often question motives and behavior. Most people recognize that we are different. However, truly recognizing and understanding the cardinal points of the Social Compass can benefit people in many aspects. We can decrease miscommunication, which decreases wasted time. This can improve performance and productivity. By understanding one's motives and methods of operation, we are more likely to support a higher level of morale, which also builds the team's success.

This chapter explores the four dispositional styles. It offers an understanding of personalities, communication, and behavioral choices. It is meant to compliment the profiles that you may have taken or stand alone if you have not taken an assessment. Your Social Compass is developed so you can utilize this information to excel in leading teams and managing various projects.

Within several chapters, we will address some of the most commonly asked questions and challenges posted to me by project managers and team leaders across the United States. A couple of the challenges and questions addressed in this chapter include:

"As a project manager, how can I gain an understanding of different personalities and communication styles among team members? How can I coach, mentor and motivate them?"

The Winner is always part of the answer.
The Loser is always part of the problem.
The Winner always has a program.
The Loser always has an excuse.
The Winner says, "Let me do it for you."
The Loser says, "That's not my job."
The Winner sees an answer for every problem.
The Loser sees a problem for every answer.
The Winner sees a green near every sand trap
The Loser sees two or three sand traps near every green.
The Winner says, "It may be difficult but it's possible."
The Loser says, "It might be possible but it's too difficult."
Be a Winner.
--Vince Lombardi

The Navigator

As we discussed previously, the Navigator is the type that correlates most closely with leadership. This behavioral style embraces competition, control, and achievement. They are no-nonsense people who embrace risk in the name of success and goal attainment. Depending on their position, Navigators thrive in situations where they are in control. They prefer to take orders from one authority: Themselves.

This type is able to make unpopular decisions for the sake of the project's success. They are confident in the risks they take and the decisions they make. This may be because Navigators have a keen sense of the big picture. They often have an uncanny ability to see three or four steps ahead, when many others are still analyzing the issue before them.

In this, Navigators are very time focused. When working with a Navigator, many realize that this type expects the work due today to be completed yesterday. Part of this expectation may be because they see what "can be" and know the timeframe to make the possibility real. If you work for a Navigator, it may be very apparent that timeliness and punctuality are critical components to the team.

Furthermore, Navigators move, think, and speak quickly. They seem to constantly be in-motion, on the go, or driving momentum. When looking at their schedule, others may sense that there is never a moment's rest. Because of the perception of constantly being in-demand, many individuals hesitate to bring pertinent issues to the table of the Navigator. They may fear that the leader is too busy to listen, to act, or to objectively work on the problem. When a Navigator is under a great deal of pressure and does not have the time to listen, act, or resolve an issue, he may lash out due to frustration or become extremely controlling and rigid. In this situation, few people have the confidence or skills to effectively work with a Navigator. This hesitancy can lead to severe problems in the future.

On the topic of communication, Navigators tend to be very open. By that, I mean they tend to be brutally honest and openly offer their opinion on the subject (whether asked or not). People whose style lies with this preference are naturally assertive, and sometimes overtly aggressive. They are not in their position because they won a popularity contest, but because they were able to make a difficult decision for the good of the project or the team. Again, this leads back to their ability to see the grand picture and keep connected to the vision they embrace.

In addition, Navigators are natural leaders. This means they have a wonderful magnetic style which attracts those who need leadership. They often display qualities of charisma and fortitude, which naturally influence others to strive towards the same goal. They enjoy influencing others, and can do so with little effort. This may be a critical element in encouraging followers to move in a direction that may not be comfortable or familiar, but may be necessary for growth, for survival, or for success.

Navigators are also very competitive and are motivated for greatness. Many of them enjoy the visual rewards and trophies their hard work brings. Frequently, Navigators may display or own power symbols as a reminder to them for all they have accomplished and as a tip to others that they are successful.

This motivation for greatness may be another reason why so many others flock to them for guidance and leadership. People want to be a part of success and of greatness. Navigators see the possibilities and, through their competitive nature, can direct others to pool their efforts towards the vision and achievements of success.

Navigators embrace honesty. They expect everyone to understand and do their part without intervention or assistance. They work hard and lead harder. They have high expectations and the assertive qualities to reach those expectations. Their vision is extraordinary, and their longing for achievement is strong.

Famous Navigators

You probably could picture several Navigators while reading the typical traits of this style. Many of the famous Navigators were also leaders, some successful, some not. Some of the more obvious Navigators of time include: Franklin D. Roosevelt, Jack Welch, Harry Truman, Adolph Hitler, Rudy Giuliani, Pat Summit, and General Patton.

When you look at the influence these people have had on others, the results inspired, the competitive nature they housed, the opinions they offered, and the masses they led, you can see in each of them the qualities of a Navigator.

As you can see, not everyone who is a Navigator leads their people in a positive direction. Hitler had such a presence that he was able to inspire millions of people to accomplish one of the most devastating and horrific goals known to mankind. Was he a Navigator? Yes.

On the other hand, when you study Navigators like Presidents Truman or FDR, or Jack Welch, and Mayor Giuliani, you will see the many positive things a great Navigator can accomplish. Each of these noble men led groups in times that were tough. They not only were able to see the big picture, but were able to navigate their teams and nations through the trials and tribulations of the time. They positively transformed companies, cities, and nations while overcoming one obstacle after another. They had a powerful, constructive and successful vision. They shared that vision with others. Their people bought into that vision and made it real. They were competitive, strong willed and charismatic decision makers. They navigated their people through storms, lulls, and sunny days. They are Navigators.

Many of you may be wondering... "OK, I understand their nature: Strive for results, honor time, be logical, spur a quick pace... but what are some of the signs to recognize a Navigator in a meeting if I don't already know this person? I can't give personality profiles to every person I bump into! How can I communicate with a Navigator if this is not my preferred style? What are the strengths and stressors for this type? How can I improve my team and decrease the negative impact of the stressors for the Navigator type?"... Fear not, each of these will be discussed in detail in future chapters.

Leadership can be thought of as a capacity to define oneself to others in a way that clarifies and expands a vision of the future ~ Edwin H. Friedman

Summary of the Navigator Preference

Qualities and Traits

➤ Motivated by results, achievement, accomplishment and success
➤ Take-charge, bottom-line focus
➤ Visionaries
➤ Time-conscientious
➤ Thrive when given the reigns and allowed to feel in control
➤ Assertive, and at times, aggressive
➤ Influential and charismatic
➤ Strong-willed and opinionated
➤ Hard working, possibly even work-aholics
➤ May be perceived as bossy, uncaring, or intimidating
➤ Competitive and goal-driven
➤ Works well when in charge or does not have to constantly answer to anyone
➤ Works well when others work independently and without many questions or need for supervision
➤ Risk takers for the sake of excellence
➤ Typically, more reserved with personal information
➤ Enjoys recognition, awards, limelight
➤ Tend to focus more on the project than on the team members' opinions and feelings
➤ Use thinking words and logic versus emotional context
➤ Makes decisions easily

Story of a Navigator

"Shirley, get Ted on the line. Oh, and I am heading to the airport, I will be back Friday night. You have my cell if you need anything. What? Oh, yes connect him." Larry was on the phone handling business while in the taxi on the way to the airport. His briefcase was full and his schedule was hectic. "Ted, Larry. Does 10:00 still work? Right. See you then." He sat back and looked at his watch. The flight leaves in 2 hours. In that time, he will keep on the phone and connect with as many people as he can.

At the airport, he noticed several lines for his departing airline baggage check-in. He checked his watch again. He can either wait in a longer line indoors or wait behind two people at the paid curbside baggage. Which is faster? Which will get him there first? He decided to check in baggage at the curb so he can get to security faster.

While heading to security, his phone rang again. "Larry here. Hey Gene. Hand ball? When? Doubles? Against whom? Oh, a wager, that would make it worthwhile! Count me in."

In line at security, he grew impatient. He began eyeing the other lines to see which was moving. He made a bet with himself that his line would move faster. Then, the woman in front of him stopped and started talking to a friend. They were deep in some emotional-driven touchy-feely conversation and not paying attention to the line. "Oh, jeez" he thought, "move!" He was just about to cut in front of them when they looked up and moved through the metal detector.

This is Larry's life. It may be viewed as typical behavior for the Navigator type.

The Social Servitor

The Social Servitor is by far the most personable of the four cardinal points. These folks love to talk to others, to connect with friends, to share stories with individuals, and to meet new people. Their behavior style embraces communication, cooperation, team work and connection. They thrive in settings where they can be of service to others, where they can visit with other people, where they can develop their personal and professional interests, and where they can be creative.

While they may support the Navigator's lead, these two types often do not see eye-to-eye. On the one hand, Navigators may make difficult (and often unpopular) decisions. On the other hand, Social Servitors prefer a more democratic means of making decisions. They prefer to consider the thoughts and emotions of all individuals involved. Their focus is much more people-based whereas the Navigator's focus is much more project -based.

In addition, the Social Servitors are very team oriented. When working with a Social Servitor, many realize these types expect the group to be considered first. Conversations for a decision may take more time, as Social Servitors prefer to get the input of each member before a decision is made. If you work for a Social Servitor, you may be very well aware of the devotion to team cohesion.

Furthermore, Social Servitors tend to reflect and think before making a decision or acting on information. They are not as quick paced as are Navigators, and seem to be more approachable than their opposites.

It is not uncommon for people who work with Social Servitors to be more comfortable with unscheduled conversations and open-door policies. These social servants excel when their cohorts, supervisors and subordinates are comfortable enough to stop in unexpectedly and visit. The conversations may be about work-related issues, team morale, or personal circumstances. This enhances concepts of trust, loyalty and commitment, but may impede timely completion of projects and tasks. This stressful situation may be due to the fact that Social Servitors find it difficult to say no to others, even if it means putting their needs and projects last.

Besides the social connection for this type, Social Servitors also need to creatively express themselves. Many with this dispositional style are motivated by creativity. This may include painting, writing, gardening, designing, or other means of expression. Unlike Explorers, this is not necessarily a constant drive. Often for Social Servitors, this creative drive will fluctuate. Some people may feel the need for creative expression for months at a time, and others will feel this need for just a few weeks every couple of years.

In addition to this need for expression, the Social Servitor has a tremendous drive for emotional well being. They speak in terms of feelings instead of thought, they naturally empathize and sympathize with others, and they are sometimes construed as overly sensitive. It is this sensitivity that encourages group cohesion, team productivity and departmental morale.

In part of their innate connection to the group, Social Servitors are typically optimistic and less formal than their Navigator counterparts. They embrace positive attitudes in the workplace and at home. Being that the people are more important to them than the project details, they also place emphasis on keeping those people happy.

> *But friendship is precious, not only in the shade, but in the sunshine of life; and thanks to a benevolent arrangement of things, the greater part of life is sunshine.* ~ Thomas Jefferson

In order to do this, Social Servitors spend a great deal of time listening to others. This disposition has tremendous listening skills. Their warm, caring and earnest personality encourages situations in which their listening skills are fully appreciated. The Social Servitor has a knack for reading between the lines, for recognizing the unspoken message, and for acting on that active listening gift to make people feel more comfortable.

Along the same lines, these types like to be heard. They enjoy talking and thinking aloud. Brainstorming with others is rejuvenating and it encourages that spark of creativity. Communication is important to them. Without it, they may feel depressed, lost, or without purpose.

Coinciding with this need for connection is the need for recognition. For the Social Servitor, this may be a genuine public recognition. They do not prefer the trophies or power symbols like the Navigators do. They prefer open and earnest recognition that confirms they are valuable and appreciated.

Famous Social Servitors

While reading these typical traits, you could probably picture several people you know who may prefer this disposition. There have been many famous Social Servitors in our time. While these celebrities have not taken the Social Compass, it may seem likely that the following Social Servitors include Abraham Lincoln, Jimmy Carter, Princess Diana, and Mother Theresa.

When you look at how these people listen, communicate, serve others, and express creativity, there may be no doubts that they have Social Servitor preferences. Granted, many of these were also leaders and influencers, however their method of leading others was (or is) much more democratic, sensitive, and encouraging than those who have a strong Navigator preference.

These people were (and still are) also fantastic communicators. They made others feel comfortable enough to share the most personal and important issues. They encourage reflection, insight, and development of those with whom they interact. They offer programs that embrace creativity and expression. They are powerful because they empower others through their soft-skills.

> *Let us be grateful to people who make us happy; they are the charming gardeners who make our souls blossom.*
> ~ *Marcel Proust*

Summary of the Social Servitor Preference

Qualities and Traits

- Motivated by connection, team cohesion, belonging, and love
- Democratic, focus on personal-well-being
- Communicators
- Feelings-conscientious
- Thrive when allowed to socialize and serve others
- Caring, genuine, and earnest about helping others
- Influential and charismatic
- Thoughtful and optimistic
- May be perceived as overly sensitive, wishy-washy, or pushovers,
- Personable and team-driven
- Works well when working with others, and allowed to creatively grow and develop
- Works well when others take time to communicate, reflect and cooperate as a team
- Service to others for the sake of the group
- More enthusiastic with personal information
- Enjoys recognition and appreciation
- Tend to focus more on the people than on the project
- Use feeling words versus logical, reserved context
- Skilled listeners

Story of a Social Servitor

Jennifer laughed as the students around her shared stories about their winter break. "Ms. Korsoff, what did you do on break?" "Oh," she replied with an eager reserve, "we went south to Atlanta to visit our family and take in some sun." The energy in her class room was high, conversational, and informal, and she enjoyed every moment that she connected with the students.

Later in the day, the principal cornered Jennifer in the hall. "Jennifer, we are desperate for a sponsor for Student Council. I know you are coaching and involved in the musicals, but the kids love you and I think you would be good for this group. You are kind, genuine, a great listener and would make a great model for these students." Jennifer looked at him with a smile on her face, but with mixed emotions under that smiling mask. *Gosh, the time involved is so great,* she thought. *I am just getting things in order. I really can't...* she thought. Jennifer then looked at the principal and, while glancing away, said with a reserved tone, "I dunno. I am awfully busy.. What are the feelings of the other teachers and students" He interrupted her, "They all feel you would be a great sponsor and actually recommended you. Can you do it for the kids?" She sighed heavily and said, "I'll think about it." He smiled and as he returned to his office said, "Great Jennifer, the group will be so happy to hear that!"

Jennifer just couldn't say no. She wanted to please everyone and wanted to belong in the greatest levels. This is much like a Social Servitor. They enjoy sharing stories with others, listening to others, helping others, and belonging to various groups.

The Explorer

The Explorer type does just what the name represents: explores. They are tremendous trouble shooters because they see things from different perspectives. This behavioral style embraces freedom, innovation, and challenges. They are free-willed and spirited people who support change for the sake of newness. Explorers thrive in situations where they can maintain a sense of independence and autonomy. They prefer to start several projects, but once the luster of newness wears off, they tend to become bored with the details and perhaps the project itself.

This type is able to think outside the box. They are confident in their creative strengths and are often sought for this particular reason. They are also great visionaries, much like Navigators. In this, they typically bore with attention to details. If the conversation revolves around intricate or technical specifics, they may lose focus and mentally wander from the conversation towards more exciting thoughts.

Unlike the Navigator type, most Explorers rarely attend to time in such a passionate manner. In fact, unless required by the work environment, few Explorers opt to wear or own a watch. If you work for an Explorer, you may notice that they do not consider time, but they do consider creative energy to be a critical component of the team.

Like the Navigator type, Explorers move, think and speak quickly. However, their speech and language is less formal than that of the Navigator. While the Navigator expects brief, succinct, and logical conversations, the Explorers invite informal, energetic, and creative conversations. Like the Social Servitor, they often share their experiences and invite similar casual communication. They are also extremely optimistic and enthusiastic, and they attempt to rub this spirit onto those around them.

While the Explorers enjoy stimulating and entertaining conversation, they may not have the patience that coincides with the tremendous listening abilities of the Social Servitor. Often, the Explorer's conversation will jump from topic to topic, and they become frustrated when others can not follow suit or do not speak at a quick pace. Along the same lines, they may appear to have a sense of chaos and disorder about them, but many Explorers note that this active environment spurs the very change and creativity they seek.

> *One of the advantages of being disorderly is that one is constantly making exciting discoveries.* ~ A. A. Milne

Explorers can also be very opinionated in conversation, much like the Navigator. They can be brutally honest with little regard to the other's emotional well being. They can also take criticism, but may be more apt to rebel against the messenger than a Navigator might.

This free-spirited disposition also has a tremendous need for action and adventure. They will explore whatever they possibly can out of the sheer joy of discovery. Many of these Explorers open everyone else's eyes to new possibilities, new solutions, and new products. By encouraging exploration of new ideas, the Explorers feed their need for intellectual adventure. However, they also crave emotional, physical, and spiritual adventure as well. Much of their off time may be devoted to satisfying these needs.

When working with an Explorer, know they thrive when they are left to actively work on their own. They feel suffocated when micromanaged and often view this as a lack of trust. This may stifle their creativity and loyalty to the project. If they are your supervisor, they expect you to also be able to work on your own, to visit with them freely, to explore new ideas together, and to respect innovation.

Explorers are action-oriented and do not necessarily enjoy the details behind a project's maintenance. They seem to appreciate it when they can voice their opinions, brainstorm new and creative ideas, and then leave the details and maintenance phase to the Workers and other types. Explorers enjoy putting the vision to action and leaving the specifics to people who love those very particulars.

Famous Explorers

As reading through these qualities, you may have thought of some Explorer people you know. These individuals are extremely colorful in nature and nearly unforgettable. They provide great fresh energy and tremendous zest to the team. There are many famous Explorers as well. Some of the more obvious Explorers include: Benjamin Franklin, Christopher Columbus, Mark Twain, Tracy Ullman, Charlie Chaplin and Dolly Parton.

As you can see, each of these Explorers discovered new ways of doing things, new sights, new nations, or new products. They rebelled against monotony and structure at one point or another. They were colorful and extremely innovative in their thinking. They began several projects and encouraged Worker types to care for the doldrums of details once all was in place. Each of these famous Explorers shaped a bit of history by their earnest zeal for life and adventure. It was their creative, confident vision that spurred Navigators to steer in the direction of that goal. It was their tremendous enthusiasm and belief in their ideas that spurred much of their work towards success. Without our Explorer types, many things would be very different than they are today.

> *Everything can be taken from a man but ... the last of the human freedoms - to choose one's attitude in any given set of circumstances, to choose one's own way.*
> ~ *Victor Frankl*

Summary of the Explorer Preference

Qualities and Traits

➤ Motivated by adventure, freedom, and excitement
➤ Independent, innovative focus
➤ Visionaries
➤ Thrive when given creative reign and allowed to feel in control
➤ Assertive, optimistic, and outgoing
➤ Influential and charismatic
➤ Strong-willed and opinionated
➤ Relaxed, comfortable, and open communication style
➤ May be perceived as opinionated, unorganized rebellious, or flighty
➤ Change-driven
➤ Works well when working as an independent or is not constantly micromanaged
➤ Works well when others work independently and without many questions or need for supervision
➤ Risk takers for the sake of newness
➤ Very extroverted and social
➤ Enjoys time off, travel and recognition
➤ Extremely creative thinkers, fantastic troubleshooters and supporters of new options
➤ Bores easily with extreme details, routine, or inflexibility

Story of an Explorer

One afternoon, Linda was preparing for an appointment she had. She had packed all of her things in a nice, tidy system. She looked around at her order in her home office and was pleased with the structure she built for herself.

Gary, Linda's husband, came flying through the house. He beamed at her as he held up an odd tool. "Look, honey," he proclaimed with pride, "I found the part we needed to fix the sink!" Linda looked at Gary and just smiled and said, "Great! Did you finish cleaning out the back room?" Gary replied with enthusiasm, "Not yet, I found this and was so thrilled, I had to show you. I will clean it before you come back."

Linda left for her appointment, on time.

Gary, on the other hand, was so excited with his find, that all he could focus on was fixing the bathroom sink. He tried to finish cleaning the back room, but this new project was constantly on his mind. He finally resolved to work on the bathroom sink instead of the back room.

When Linda came home, there were boxes and toiletries all over the floor. She shook her head in amazement. "Gary! What happened!? Gary?" "In here, honey" she heard him reply. She followed the trail to the bathroom, where Gary was sitting, staring at the sink. "I just had to fix the sink" Gary replied. "I found some of these supplies we had on our list, so I took them out. Man, I'm tired. Let's take a break." Linda shook her head. She knew of Gary's habit to have three or four projects started at once, and the likelihood that few of them will get finished within a reasonable time frame. This eagerness and behavior may be typical of Explorer types.

The Worker

The Worker type is very task conscientious. This type connects closely to terms like "worker bee" and "workaholic". They want to focus on the details and get the job done right. When they are finished, many times they request additional projects as a reward for finishing the previous tasks. They are truly task-oriented.

This type is able to see the minute details required to make the big picture a reality. When people want to hurry through to the end result, the Workers are the ones who bring the vision to earth by attending to the specifics. Without these diligent individuals, the greater picture would be very difficult to attain.

Much like the Navigators, the Worker type is very results focused. When working with a Worker, recognize they will expect things to be accomplished properly. This is a strong drive for them, and if something unexpected happens to delay the results or to cause change, Worker types may become frustrated. For this reason, many individuals dread visiting with Worker types when it comes to change. They may not want to face the frustrated reactions that these dependable people may have. Worker types are thinkers and prefer thinking about a situation before change or postponed deadlines are decided.

In addition, Worker types are much more deliberate in thought, movement and speech. Just like their uncanny eye for details, the Worker types have a natural drive to "chew on things" before answering or coming to a decision. This is very different from the Explorer types, who typically make very quick decisions and then think about those decisions later.

This speed also transcends into dialogue. Worker types are more reserved in conversation. They may be less likely to express their opinion or to voluntarily share stories of themselves. In this, they also prefer the more formal means of communication. This is very different from the Explorer or Social Servitor dispositions, where open and less formal conversational methods are preferred.

In their world of logic, Workers are extremely analytical and abiding citizens. Before making decisions, they may refer to the procedural guidelines. Rarely will a Worker type make a decision before addressing regulations, logic, and specifics of all the options. This means they also request all of this information from others so they can make an informed and intelligent decision. With this in mind, Workers do enjoy making decisions and being involved in the decision making process.

In working with others, the Worker enjoys the company of individuals who appreciate hard work and logical thinking. They do not mind team work, as long as the effort is without drama or change and everyone pulls their own weight. Like Social Servitors, those with the Worker disposition are not comfortable with conflict. Be certain to consider the Worker types' personal interest in their projects when you offer correction or give feedback.

Additionally, the Worker types are creative in a very logical manner. In fact, it is my experience that every one of these four cardinal types has some connection to creativity. The type of creativity and how it is expressed is what varies among these four preferred styles. For the Worker type, this creativity is much more centered:

focused on the details of a project, around the logic of an invention, and around the joy of creating something that works in its perfection. Thomas Edison is a prime example of this type of creative individual.

Similar to the Navigator type, Worker types are extremely goal driven and strive for greatness. However, the greatness they desire is more of a perfection in details and a tie to their project than of a recognized success and achievement. When these two dispositions meet, you truly have a hard-working individual who will not think twice about working 60 or more hours per week to accomplish the desired goals.

The dictionary is the only place that success comes before work. Hard work is the price we must pay for success. I think you can accomplish anything if you're willing to pay the price. ~ Vince Lombardi

Famous Workers

Who do you know that fits the typical Worker behavioral preference? Many of the famous Workers were catalysts of their time. The hard work, dedication, and attention to detail helped perfect many wonderful advances we have today. Some of the more obvious Worker types include: Thomas Edison Sherlock Holmes, Tony La Russa, Meryl Streep, and characters like Gil Grissom of CSI.

When you look at their thought process, their joy in their approaches and methods to find answers, their thirst for knowledge and details, and their logic, you can see this type's behavioral preferences. They are the catalysts to accomplishments, to goal attainment, and to diligence all around them. When you look at the methods each used when attacking their project (whether finding the suspect or finding the answers), you can see in each of them their unique creativity, their love for details and their connection to thought. In this, you may also get a greater understanding of their working principles when dealing with others.

These people have positively transformed the world as we know it. This did not happen out of influence or assertive behaviors. This happened out of internal conversation, out of joy for progress, and out of a sense of stability. They have an independent vision that they link to the whole. They are competitive with themselves, striving with perfection in specifics and taking pride in their end products.

The Worker types work through chaotic tempests. They thrive and seek structure. In a storm of chaos, Workers will make a stable, solid world for themselves. They will continue to work hard and get the job done in hopes that the storm will settle and the environmental stability will return.

> *Genius is one percent inspiration and ninety-nine percent perspiration.* ~ *Thomas Alva Edison*

Summary of the Worker Preference

Qualities and Traits

➤ Motivated by details, goal achievement, results and stability
➤ Focus on specifics and details
➤ Project-oriented
➤ Time-conscientious
➤ Thrive when working in structured , thinking environment
➤ Reserved and reflective
➤ Dependable and reliable
➤ Hard working, possibly even work-aholics
➤ May be perceived as inflexible, rigid and even too attached to the specifics
➤ Dedicated and goal-driven
➤ Works well when left to work on the project with few changes or with a detailed description of changes
➤ Works well when others work diligently and get their task accomplished on time
➤ Toilers and workers for the sake of excellence and goal achievement
➤ Introverted, logical and thoughtful
➤ Enjoys quiet recognition of a job well done, additional projects, and an appreciation of their hard work and thoroughness
➤ Tend to focus more on the project than on the team members' opinions and feelings
➤ Use thinking words and logic versus emotional context

A Story of a Worker Type

Upon visiting my brother in Austin, TX, I was reminded how detail-oriented he truly was. My brother can be thought of as the epitome of the Worker disposition.

After he picked me up from the airport one hot Sunday afternoon, he informed me that we HAD to stop at the auto parts store before heading to his house. This was no surprise to me. It is the only store my brother will eagerly frequent. He is an automobile fan, having built a race car and constantly rebuilding cars he finds. This is not his job, but it is his passion.

At the auto store, we stopped in to find two products: an exterior tar-remover, and a detailer product. Most people may casually inspect the items and choose a product with little additional thought. My brother, and many Worker types, are not like this.

When he found the tar remover (he uses the same product all the time, no matter what sales are running), he then methodically eyed all of the detailer options. Some were on sale, others were not. He opened each brand, smelled each one, closed the bottles and stepped back, cautiously eyeing the products. He then inspected each's ingredients list, comparing each to the other. Additionally, he noted the price and calculated how much each bottle was per ounce. He finally chose a brand and headed towards the payment counter. His tall 6 foot 4 inch frame stopped suddenly and he looked back with his large, brown eyes and said, "I don't know." He then sauntered back to the detailer products and went through the entire process again. He finally settled on the product he originally chose and paid with confidence. This attention to detail is a true behavior of many Worker types.

Similarities and Differences

Some of these dispositions share similar characteristics. The compass allows variance and degrees of adjustment. This section will explore the similarities and differences between the cardinal points. Remember, people typically do have some of each of these qualities. However, more often than not, individuals have a very strong preference (or two) that come naturally, and the strengths of the other styles are not as natural.

Navigator and Worker

Both Navigator types and Worker types work towards goal attainment. They both are respectful of time and deadlines (although the Worker type may need a reminder, as they can get "lost" in the details and need for perfection). Each type may be more formal than the Social Servitors or Explorer types. In addition, both think in terms of logic and project. So how are they different?

The Navigator and Worker types are different in that the Navigator is very influential and outgoing in opinion and attitude. The Worker type is much more reserved and does not approach the leadership styles in the same way that Navigator types may. In addition, Navigator types tend towards outward recognition and announcement of achievements and status quo. The Worker types may prefer a more individualized reward and may keep their achievements at a more personal level. Furthermore, Worker types respond well to additional work and responsibilities as a reward. For the Navigator, these are also sought, but more for the status quo than for the task itself. In addition, the Navigator type may be more open to risk and change, whereas the Worker type is more comfortable with security and stability. Another difference is the tendency towards the big picture for Navigators and towards the details for Workers.

Navigator and Explorer

Just as the Navigator styles and Worker styles share similarities and differences, so do the Navigator and Explorer types.

Both the Navigator and Explorer types tend to be more flamboyant and opinionated in nature. Neither seems to care what others think of them or their decisions. Both of these styles wish others would do the work, and do it "my" way. The similarities with these types lie in their energy, in their attitude, and in their desire to take risks. Both styles think, act, and speak quickly and bore with lengthy or detailed conversation when they are not in control.

So, how are the Navigator type and the Explorer type different? They are different in regards to the means of task accomplishment. Typically, the Navigator type is much more focused, driven, and centered on the project. The Explorer type tends to explore many options at once, not necessarily concerned with whether or not these projects are completed on time. The Navigator type is highly respectful of time and a hard work ethic, whereas the Explorer type may appear to be respectful of freedom and newness. The Navigator type tends to think in terms of logic and project, and the Explorer type tends to think in terms of intuition and process.

Explorer and Social Servitor

These two styles share many similarities and still are very different. For instance, both are very optimistic and friendly in nature. Both are frustrated with views that only address the project and not the people or the process. The Explorer type is highly creative. The Social Servitor is also creative, but the drive for creativity is more sporadic. Both styles tend toward social well being, although their choices of socializing may differ depending on their comfort level with the environment.

With this in mind, the differences lie in their need for familiarity. In this, the Social Servitor may be more reserved in a new group than the Explorer. The Explorer typically does not care what others think and may act or react on a more extreme or flamboyant level. The Social Servitor is very aware of what others think of them, thus may approach situations with more reservation.

On the one hand, the Explorer bores easily and may spark conflict just for the excitement. On the other hand, the Social Servitor tends to shy away from personal conflict, although their ability to mediate other's conflict is tremendous. This is important to remember when dealing with conflict in the workplace.

The Explorer type seeks independence, freedom, and excitement. The Social Servitor seeks stability, belonging, and cohesion. Finally, the Explorer is very open in regards to opinion and decisions and the Social Servitor is more thoughtful and reserved in regards to opinion and decisions. Not only do each value opinions of others, they also value your attitude. They expect great attitudes!

Social Servitor and Worker

Along the same regards, the Social Servitor and Worker types share some similarities and differences. Some of the similarities include being more reserved than the Explorer or Navigator types. Both the Social Servitor and Worker types approach new situations or groups with greater caution. The Social Servitor and the Worker type tend to take criticism personally, thus the feedback provided to each of these types requires some thought and care. Additionally, these types are not fond of personal conflict and may tend to vent the issues with outsiders instead of facing those directly involved.

So, their similarities lie in the reserved and cautious process of action. What are the differences? The differences lie in the thought process and focus. Worker types tend to focus on the project, whereas the Social Servitor types tend to focus on the people. The Worker types think in terms of linear concepts and logic, and the Social Servitor types think in terms of team and feelings. The Social Servitor may be able to focus on details, but not to the extent that the Worker types do. When speaking to Social Servitors, they prefer language that incorporates people, feelings, and process. When speaking to Workers, they prefer language that incorporates fact, details, and project.

These comparative lists are not final, and you may have additional similarities or differences in mind. As basic as this list is, it is important to remember these qualities when working with others, recognizing their preferred style, and adjusting to speak their language.

Dynamic Dispositions

On a compass, there are four directions (N, S, E, and W). Between each of those cardinal points are markers that note variations of degree. Sometimes, people need to head SW in order to reach their destination most effectively. For instance, let's say you live in Buffalo, NY and you would like to visit Amarillo, TX. If you headed south you may end up near Spartanburg, SC and then have to head due west to Amarillo. With this direction, you could still get the "job" done, but it would take much more time, energy and resources. By being flexible and heading SW, you could reach Amarillo with less time, energy, resources and human effort.

As mentioned earlier, research notes that approximately 30% of a project manager's and team leader's time is spent correcting miscommunication. When I recite this information to the project managers and team leaders, they laugh and note, "I thought that statistic would be higher!" This reaction speaks volumes.

With this in mind, it is important to remember that people are dynamic. There are many situations that require individuals to adjust behavioral style in order to communicate the message as accurately as possible. This accuracy does not mean just checking the message, but how the message is delivered. Remember, people are not one dimensional. We fluctuate between these cardinal dispositions as the situation allows. However, we each typically have one preferred style that may be a great influence over our communication and behavior. Some common mixes of styles are explored more in this section.

NE

Some individuals may be equally comfortable with the Navigator-Explorer styles. This means they have either the Navigator or Explorer dominant characteristics, but often relate very easily to the additional style's qualities (perhaps on the Social Compass profile, the Explorer type and the Navigator type scores are close together). Many innovative, creative, and spitfire leaders fall into this category. They are highly energetic, charismatic, adventurous, and inspired. They love their freedom, appreciate the creativity of others, and are competitive as well as fun loving. It is a combination of assertiveness, of spontaneity, of vision, and of energy. They expect timely accomplishments and may be perceived as overly aggressive or arrogant due to their tremendous enthusiasm, confidence, and sometimes rebellious nature.

NW

Other individuals may be comfortable with both the Navigator and the Worker styles. This means they have either the Navigator or Worker dominant characteristics, but often easily relate to the additional style's qualities. These two scores on the Social Compass may be very close together.

For instance, this type may consist of many hard-nosed, workaholic, process driven individuals. This means these people are truly project oriented with little natural forethought to the people involved. They are heavily guided by deadlines, bottom lines, and staying within the lines. They proceed by the book, dot all their i's and cross all their t's. They are extremely goal-oriented and have high expectations, not only for themselves but for others.

SE

This combination of traits is an interesting one. People who are comfortable with both the Social Servitor and the Explorer types are very enthusiastic, optimistic, friendly and outgoing. They have a strong attraction because of their energy. They have an intense need for creative outlets, for personal connection, for informal conversations, and for being needed. They may seem flighty, chatty, or even a little "dingy" by those who do not understand their wonderful strengths and inherent weaknesses. They use terms relating to team, people, and feelings more than NE, or NW types might. They have a tremendous zeal for life and want to share that with the world, whether the world (i.e. NW types) wants it or not!

SW

Those people who are comfortable with both the Social Servitor and the Worker styles work hard and prefer working with others. They pay attention to the specifics and consider people as much as the project. They remain time- and goal-oriented. With regards to criticism, they may take it more personally than other types, so the method of feedback should be considered before it is offered. They enjoy belonging to groups and feeling as if they have served others well. They do have a sense of creativity; however, it is more internal and unique than a SE's might be. While they enjoy, and need, the company of others, they are much more reserved and selective in their companionships. This is also different from the SE's. They work hard, have a strong sense of loyalty, and hope (or expect) the same in return.

Polar Opposites

Of course, people would not be people if we did not have the attraction of opposites. This not only works when opposite personalities attract, but also when opposite behavioral styles are preferred by one individual.

For instance, when people prefer both the Navigator and the Social Servitor styles (being a NS), they may be great democratic leaders. In this, they have a great sense of vision and how that vision relates to the people on their team. They are more assertive than typical Social Servitors and are much more people-oriented than typical Navigator types. They continue to be magnetic in nature, with a great sense of loyalty and group cohesion. NS dispositions are still competitive, but attend to the sportsmanship that coincides with tactful competition. They focus on goals, and are drawn into objectives that relate to their group as a unit. Their communication styles may be more open to informal and timely conversation than that of a NW. These types are great influencers and have a tremendous ability to get a team in motion.

The other polar opposite is the EW type. This genuine type is not as common as the other types, but it is a type that some people naturally exhibit. In this, individuals are comfortable with both the Explorer and the Worker types. They work hard and play hard. They may attend to details and specifics in their job (the Worker preference) but their off-time may include more adventure and freedom (the Explorer type). They may get bored with mundane tasks, but they do not quit. They complete a project as required, even if their rebellious side begs them to set it aside for a day of entertainment. They are time driven when it applies to them, and can easily forget the clock when the situation appeals to them. Did I mention they work hard and play harder?

Conclusion

These four dispositions are the cardinal points to your Social Compass. They are not stagnant, but are dynamic, just like people. Much of the time, we wonder how people will react in a situation that pertains to us. Remember, Mischel (1968) supported this in his principle: Behavior = Personality x Perception. This chapter has reviewed the behavioral preferences of each of these styles. These preferences are based on one's innate personality (introverted or extroverted? thinking or feeling?), as well as one's typical perception of situations. With this understanding, we have a greater sense of the typical actions for each style within the work or social setting.

Knowing of these different dispositions may not be enough to promote performance or work place cohesion. It is also important to recognize the various strengths and stressors that coincide with each dominant style. These next chapters will discuss the various strengths and stressors (areas of improvement) for each behavioral and communication preference.

> *As we let our own light shine, we unconsciously give other people permission to do the same. As we are liberated from our fear, our presence liberates others. ~ Marianne Williamson*

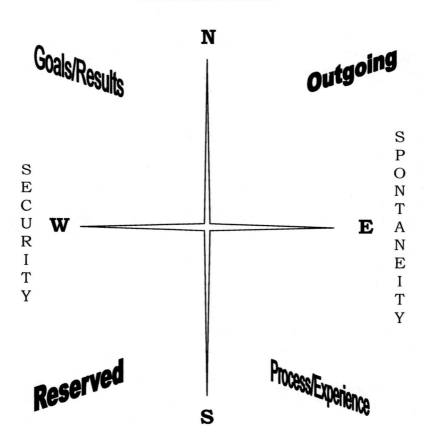

Chapter Three
Strengths

Each cardinal type has innate gifts that the other dispositions may have to work harder to achieve. We each have natural tendencies that contribute to a strong team. If every one of us thought the same way, reacted in the same manner, proceeded with the same methods, or had the same strengths, we may not be as advanced as we are today. To truly excel, we need to rely on the diverse strengths housed within each individual. We not only need to recognize those differences, but we need to embrace them.

Being human, we also have stressors that can negatively affect our performance if we do not attend to them. What some individuals may consider to be an exciting adventure, others may consider to be extremely stressful and even disturbing. Our personalities may impact how we perceive an event and that perception can lead to various intensities of stress. Distress may lead to poor work performance, a lagging relationship, or low self esteem. It is important to recognize the natural stressors or weaknesses for each preferred style so that those areas may be improved. These stressors are explored in Chapter Four.

> *The world makes way for the man who knows where he is going. ~ Ralph Waldo Emerson*

What Are Your Strengths?

Each particular disposition has strengths that contribute to success in performance, in relationships, in team cohesion, and in many other aspects of life. Often, when looking back at the most consistent actions of past, individuals may begin to truly understand their strengths and recognize their stressors. When people are unaware of their natural strengths, others around them may easily point out those qualities.

It is also interesting to note that people may frequently have a very different view about themselves and their behavior than other people may have of them. Based on this principle, there is one common exercise that many facilitators, coaches, and consultants might have clients conduct. It is simple and is outlined below:

1. Take several moments to think back to your behaviors, actions, and preferred conversational style of past. Make one list of what you think your strengths are, and another list of what you think your stressors are, based on those steadfast actions.

2. (This one may take a little "courage")... Visit with friends, coworkers, and family members. Ask each of them to write a list of what they consider to be your strengths, and a list of what they consider to be your stressors.

3. Compare the lists others have made to your lists. Is it consistent? Do you view your strengths or stressors as being different from the strengths or stressors others have listed? What do these lists tell you about your behavior in different

settings? What can you do to enhance those strengths and minimize your stressors?

This is a very simple construct that may give some great insight to individuals. The design of asking others is the same design many corporations and consultants use in 360 degree assessment and employee feedback. Asking others of their input and viewpoint can be powerful if the feedback and method is properly conducted.

For the purposes of this exercise, the design is simple and the feedback may be very informative. It can enhance one's confidence and can offer new insight to strengths. Simply put, sometimes we overestimate our strengths. Other times, we underestimate our strengths.

While we each have had different experiences that may shape our behavior, it seems that each of the prime dispositions share innate abilities. These strengths and abilities are explored in this chapter.

Navigator

The Navigator's greatest strengths lie in the ability to lead others, even through adversity. This relies on a solid foundation of assertiveness skills, decision making abilities, competition, and a thirst for achievement.

For the Navigator, these qualities and behaviors come easily. They thrive on competition which drives them toward accomplishment and achievement. For many other dispositions, competition is stressful and leads to great anxiety or poor performance, but for the Navigator, it is a natural exhilaration.

As discussed previously, the Navigators are also visionaries. They see the big picture with great ease. This sense of foresight is a tremendous strength, as they may easily navigate past obstacles and take risks more so than the other behavioral styles. This may also lead to some frustration in that Navigators may become aggravated when others don't see the big picture as quickly as they do.

Coincidentally, Navigators also attend to the specifications of a project. They can easily weigh the big picture, the objectives and the risk against the end result. This is what differentiates them from the Explorers. Explorers can see the big picture; however, they may not naturally attend to these particulars like the Navigators do.

Navigators have tremendous hard-skill strengths as well. What does this mean, exactly? Well, these individuals have a natural ability to make difficult decisions when others may not be able to address these issues. Navigator types are typically very assertive as well, with high influence and a no-fear way of sharing information. Without proper delivery, these assertive behaviors may be construed as aggressive and this may feed conflict among team members. When Navigators do recognize these strengths and attend to "softer" assertive delivery, they may be considered as loyal, trusting, honest, and hard working leaders who will do whatever it takes to get the job done.

Additionally, this disposition leads by doing and by telling and is able to drive their team to the final goal with great charisma and natural influence. Being results-oriented, the Navigators thrive on achievement, and this is no secret! One of their greatest strengths is being able to push through the final stages to a finished product, service, or situation. Much of this behavior is modeled, for they are just as apt to do as they are to tell.

When reviewing these strengths, it may be easy to tell why Navigators are important to a team. Without them, the team may not come to decisions, may not see the big picture while attending to the bottom line, and may not push for greater performance. It is this influence and desire for accomplishment that can positively drive a team towards project deliverables and success.

> *The very essence of leadership is that you have to have a vision.*
> ~ *Theodore Hesburgh*

Social Servitor

The Social Servitors have their own unique set of strengths. While the Navigator's strengths lie more in the hard skills of behavior, the Social Servitor's strengths lie more in the soft skills of behavior. They have a natural ability to listen to others and gather not only the meaning, but also the emotional construct behind the message. These individuals are fantastic in working with others, for their greatest need is to belong.

Connecting to the tremendous listening skills, Social Servitors are typically the "glue" of a team. They attend to the ideas, thoughts and feelings of an entire group before they make a balanced decision. Because of their tremendous listening abilities, Social Servitors are also effective mediators during conflict, as long as they are not personally involved in the plot itself. They embrace harmony and are democratic. This democratic tendency is a strength that most other types have to work very hard to achieve. For the Social Servitor, it is a natural action.

Beyond working well with others, Social Servitors have great strengths within creative outlets. They may not be as constantly driven towards creativity as the Explorers may be, but they are driven to create in phases or spurts. It may be said that their creative expression has a strong connection to their emotions or to self development.

Growth for the Social Servitor is a constant quest. This desire to improve is a quality that does not drive other personalities as much as it drives the Social Servitors. Many self-help books are written for this type, because they link into the emotional aspect of one's actions as well as note the importance of improvement within a team. Social Servitors desire to improve, even if just for the sake of team cohesion. They seek to understand others in order to understand themselves, and vice-versa. It is this strength that often holds a team together and enhances the performance of other Social Servitors around them.

The Social Servitor's strengths are very different from the Navigator's strengths. The Social Servitor seeks to be of service to others, to work with others, and to belong within a group. They listen, share, and encourage two-way communication. They are more relaxed in time-structure and in this, prefer to visit first before diving into the formalities of conversation. While Navigator types may construe some of these Social Servitor behaviors as frustratingly touchy-feely, it is important to the construct of the team.

When reviewing these strengths, it may be easy to tell why Social Servitors are so important to a team. Without them, the team may not be as cohesive or as united on the vision or mission as it could be. The group may not be able to effectively work through misunderstandings and conflict. Team messages may be misconstrued without the listening skills of the Social Servitor, and the need for self- and team-development may go untapped. These behavioral and communication strengths keep a team united, enhance the performance towards the vision of the Navigators, and encourage other members toward project deliverables and success.

> *Good friends, good books and a sleepy conscience: this is the ideal life.* ~ *Mark Twain*

Explorers

The Explorer type has unique strengths that many people (particularly the Worker type) may consider to be annoying weaknesses. This is not the case.

The Explorer type has a zest for life and this enthusiastic, adventurous spirit is necessary for a well-balanced team, as well as for a well-balanced individual. From this zeal comes tremendous creativity and innovation. These qualities are great strengths to have. Without them, there would be little progress towards new technology, new methods of learning, new relationships, new careers, and new relief.

Explorers are also influential, optimistic, and informal in nature. These qualities build into the strength of connection, much like the more reserved Social Servitor. However, the Explorers are more assertive, and this can act as both a strength (if well refined) or can be a weakness (if unrefined and considered aggressive). As a strength, Explorers are able to make tough decisions while considering others involved. They are able to speak their minds with an assertive tone, and often are willing to speak for others as well because of this strength.

The Explorer types are also visionaries (although, not to the extent of the Navigator types) and this big-picture sense can take their team to a new direction. Explorers do not mind taking risks. This strength is important in progress. Without risk, we would not advance. The do not fear making mistakes. They more likely fear not taking risks or exploring new options.

Adventure for an Explorer is a constant quest. This can be within a job, a relationship, a routine, or other factors of life. Explorers are solid when it comes to adding new color or flavor to the world around them. This shake-up can spur new energy to those in the vicinity, even if the new concepts are not initially well-received. They encourage change. Sometimes, this is simply for the sake of change and may not be welcomed or necessary by all involved. Other times, the recommendation for change is for the purpose of improvement or to troubleshoot problems with the project.

This brings me to another strength of the Explorer. This disposition has an uncanny knack for troubleshooting the most difficult issues. This is because they tend to think outside the box and can envision unique opportunities necessary to resolve the issue. Without this strength on a team, many projects may be scrapped at the sign of a more unusual problem. Luckily, this is not always the case.

When reviewing these strengths, it may be easier to tell why Explorers are so important to a team. They have an infectious attitude, and most of the time, this attitude is energetic and positive. They spur tremendous creativity and embrace thinking outside the box, especially when troubleshooting issues. They seek adventure, making change possible. They encourage others to welcome change in order to achieve the goals of the project or team. These behavioral and communication strengths keep a team energized. The Explorer's strengths also encourage the start up phases that people will endure to reach a vision. The Explorer style can influence a team to move towards risk in order to reach the common goal.

> *It is better to have enough ideas for some of them to be wrong, than to be always right by having no ideas at all.*
> *~ Edward de Bono*

Workers

The Worker type has many strengths in regards to the genuine need to attend to the details of a project. These people are very project oriented, like the Navigator type, but their strength is that they focus on the details more so than the big picture. This is important to a team because someone has to attend to the specifics in order to make certain the project is accurate and successful. While many people do this (some very haphazardly), the Worker naturally and eagerly reviews these details.

Beyond the details, the Worker has another strength wherein they seem to be able to design structure out of chaos. They desire stability and will do what they can to assure it is present. Along these lines, groups need the Worker type for the purpose of setting up and following through with procedures. Because of this, some may consider the Worker type to be the "policy police" and may rebel (Explorer type!).

Because they are so focused on the project, they also have a personal desire to see it succeed. They may be noted as being the most reliable and dependable of all the types. If something needs to be accomplished in order to achieve project success, the Worker type may jump in and actually do it. The Worker type is much like the Navigator type in that they tend towards goal achievement, and will do what needs to be done to reach these objectives.

Workers are also builders. They work from beginning through end, often taking few breaks. The strength herein is their pride in work and how easily they can become engulfed in their job. When you ask a Worker type what he considers to be fantastic rewards, he may reply, "Give me another project and recognize my hard work in private." Workers feed on the process, on working one step at a time. When a project is completed, they can then take a step back and really appreciate all the detail that has gone into making the big picture vision a reality.

In this, Worker types are uniquely creative. They may think through a project, exploring every detail possible before deciding upon the route needed to achieve it. Once they have explored all the options, they may choose the option with the greatest success rate. They opt for security, although knowing risk is a part of building projects.

These strengths are necessary for a team. Worker types keep the project real. They bring the vision into steps and specifications. They recognize team boundaries and individual policies and promote them. Even though people don't always appreciate these regulations, many are in place for good reason and the Workers help to keep the group regulated in many ways. The Worker disposition is one of doing, so their modeling may inspire others to do as well. If everyone on the team actually does their role in the project, there is less chance for conflict or social loafing.

> The heights by great men reached and kept
> Were not attained by sudden flight,
> But they, while their companions slept,
> Were toiling upward in the night.
> ~ Henry Wadsworth Longfellow

Strengths Summary

As you can see, each preferred style is important to team effectiveness and the project's success. Typically, one would hope to have every style present on their team to truly embrace each of the natural strengths. However, there may be times when a group does not need all of the strengths represented. It is important to review the goals before considering team members and desired strengths for that group and task.

To be a truly effective team, it is important to recognize and accept each of these strengths that coincide with the different types. It is important to not only build the strengths one already has, but to focus attention on some of the strengths of other dispositions and work to add those strengths to their repertoire.

If a person relies strictly on natural strengths, he may not achieve the same intense greatness as that of a person who also builds unnatural strengths. To do this, it is critical we recognize which strengths we lack and address how we can build those unnatural strengths.

One of the greatest exercises to do is to think of some of the strengths that your "opposite" naturally exhibits. View this list and note how each of these strengths could help your personal or professional development. Furthermore, set a goal to develop these strengths so your personality and behavioral styles are well rounded. Once you have the goal set, it is important to design an action plan, set a reward for yourself, and tell someone of your plan. This will make goal achievement even more plausible.

Developing these unnatural strengths is not easy, but it is important if we want to be exceptional individuals. For instance, my least preferred type is the Explorer type. I recognize they have tremendous strengths in adaptability and creativity that I sometimes lack. It is my continuous goal to improve upon these qualities so they become strengths of mine as well. In this, I make a conscious effort to make changes, even for the sake of change, and to be more creative in my choices and projects. I know to be exceptional, I need to build these strengths into my repertoire. I recognize these characteristics are not natural for me and I have to work hard to make them mine. I also know these are tremendous strengths to have and I admire Explorer types for these qualities.

Chapter Four
Stressors

Many organizational psychologists have compared the effects of attending solely to one's strengths to the effects of attending to strengths and developing areas of improvement. The Center of Creative Leadership conducted studies on this issue and found that people who focus **only** on their strengths may not perform as well as people who **also** transform their weaknesses into learned strengths.

You can liken this to a volleyball player's game. For instance, if a player is great at attacking the ball, but can't cover, dig, receive, or perform defensively, then that person is not a high performance player. To truly excel, it is important to develop those defensive skills so they compliment the offensive skills. When an offensive player works at improving their defensive skills, there are greater chances for better performance, and that leads to more minutes on the court.

This is equally important in the workplace. It is critical that individuals positively improve those weaker areas. They need to develop those weaker areas into strengths. Developing these areas into strengths not only aids the team, but it enhances personal performance as well.

Stressors

One question that many project managers and team leaders have posed may relate to this chapter. This question is: *"If I could ask one question, it would be 'what are you most afraid of?'* *Project team members will tailor their communications based on anticipated reactions or consequences. The project manager needs to be aware of what each person's "filter" is, and how strong it is. Fear of communicating, especially anything that negatively impacts a project, can substantially hurt the project."*

> *If a man harbors any sort of fear, it percolates through all his thinking, damages his personality, makes him landlord to a ghost* ~ *Lloyd Douglas*

This chapter is designed to tackle those fears (or stressors) that coincide with various behavioral preferences. Our stressors typically are those roadblocks that prevent us from high performance. Stressors often decrease our performance because we do not possess the strengths to confidently or successfully handle these stressors. Because of this, another goal of this text is to address those areas of improvement. This means setting a plan to work on those characteristics so these weaker areas can become learned (or developed) strengths, and so these stressors do not impede success.

Of Mice and Men

One scene in the book *Of Mice and Men* seems to be an excellent description of the Navigator's stressor. In the book, Lenny loved to pet the little field mice he caught. Unfortunately, Lenny did not realize his own brute strength and aggressive nature. He would pet and squeeze the soft little creatures so hard that he accidentally killed them. His companion George had to constantly remind Lenny to be gentler when dealing with soft creatures.

How is this compatible with Navigators? Navigators are so focused, driven, and project oriented that they may not realize the brute strength and aggressive nature they display. This can be a demotivator. Instead of spurring the team to the final end project, this aggressive style can deter productivity due to rebelliousness or emotional disconnect. If Navigators want to enhance project performance with fewer problems, it is important for them to recognize this area of improvement and actually take steps to decrease the negative effects it may have on the project or team. In other words, when working with others, it is important to be gentler in nature. Like Lenny, they want to pet the mice, not kill them.

How are these softer-skills stressors for the Navigators? These soft skills are stressors for the Navigator because they may perceive these as distractions to the project. Some of these stressors include lengthy and personal communication, listening more than controlling a conversation, using feeling words, paraphrasing, and emphasizing people as much as project. When individuals who think along these lines (like Social Servitors) enter a Navigator's office, a common practice for Navigator types is to roll their eyes, sigh, and think, "how long will this take?" By strengthening these qualities, Navigator types will still control a situation, but do so in a manner that is comfortable for all.

Building the soft skills is critical to be the best leader possible. In motivating your team, it is important to recognize their strengths and feed into those motivators. This step includes being able to adjust your communication preference to suit the situation. We will discuss more about adjustment in Chapter Six.

Summary of Stressors

The Navigator Type

❖ Long communication, personal stories, chatter

❖ Not focusing on the project or results

❖ When others are late, not attending to deadline

❖ Indecisiveness, touchy-feely excuses

❖ Having to pour over details in explanations

Turn these stressors to strengths:

❖ Set aside time to specifically attend to lengthier communication, personal stories and chatter... It will lend itself to other individuals understanding the importance of the task.

❖ Focus on people and their part of the project so that they will be encouraged to focus on the project and results

❖ Listen to their reasoning and together form a solution to decrease or cease this tendency

❖ Attend to individuals so they are comfortable and encouraged to focus on the project

❖ Understand not everyone enjoys making decisions. Walk them through the importance of their input and decisiveness.

What Do You Think?

While the Navigators find the softer skills to be stressors, the Social Servitors find those soft skills to be great strengths. While the Social Servitor types embrace the situations that the Navigator types consider stressors, they tend to run from those situations that the Navigator types embrace.

For instance, the Navigator types are fast paced, assertive and decisive. They migrate towards competitive situations, high-adrenaline decisions, and risky ventures. Social Servitors are not comfortable with these aggressive behaviors. In fact, these situations are typically viewed as stressors for the Social Servitor.

Making a difficult, unpopular but necessary decision is hard for the Social Servitor. They strive for harmony and do not want to be the instigator of discord. In this, the assertive behaviors exhibited in the Navigator and Explorer types are the same behaviors that the Social Servitor needs to improve.

When reviewing the need for assertiveness, it is easy to see how the Social Servitor is frustrated. Mind you, assertiveness is not the only frustration for Social Servitors. They may also become stressed by the inability of others to connect personally, by doing too much for everyone else and not enough for themselves, and by the constant project pressures with little attention to the people involved.

Two things are bad for the heart... running up stairs and running down people ~ Bernard M. Baruch

Summary of Stressors
The Social Servitor Type

❖ When others use short, abrupt communication, little attention to team or personal stories

❖ When others do not focus on the team or individual feelings and perceptions

❖ When others are competitive, authoritative, and unclear regarding goals and communication

❖ When others focus solely on the project and neglect the people. which leads to conflict

❖ Aggressive, overbearing conversations that may disregard the team's morale

Turn these stressors to strengths:

❖ Recognize most others do not enjoy lengthy conversations, appreciate the difference, and keep communication brief and within reason

❖ Focus on the project and the results when considering people. Without the project, the team would not exist.

❖ Listen to their reasoning and remind yourself that you are not in competition and that it is acceptable to verify the task's action steps.

❖ Be assertive about the feelings, considerations and morale of the team. With these in play, the project's performance is heightened. Being assertive builds strengths and respect by many behavioral types.

Don't Box Me In

This is the motto of the Explorer type. They may explore the box, but only on their own terms. This free-spirited, sometimes rebellious nature has many strengths. It also carries a strong stressor and area of improvement.

While the Explorers seek adventure, freedom, and creative outlets, they seem to hide from structure, detail, and discipline. This is the greatest weakness and stressor for them.

Many Explorer types loathe regulations, routine, and micromanagement. Their lack of discipline makes it difficult to complete these types of tasks, especially when their defiant nature kicks in. In this, the weight of their desire for freedom and adventure interrupts their need to follow through with details and tasks. When this happens, they are actually disrupting and limiting their opportunities for freedom. They become tied to the very tasks and specifics they wish to flee.

To be truly "free", the Explorer disposition needs to attend to the issue of self-discipline, details, and follow-through. By building these areas into developed strengths, Explorer types may find they have more freedom, more creative outlets, and more possibilities for adventure. When the issues of self-discipline, details and follow-through are developed into strengths, they no longer continue to be heavy stressors.

When Explorers are faced with the need of self-discipline and attention to detail, they may procrastinate. In this, they are delaying the inevitable. They are also delaying the gratification and freedom that comes from completing these specifics. This "boxed in" sensation is one of dread, frustration, and often times, bitterness. However, when Explorers can gain the sense of self discipline, they are able to accomplish the tasks on time and have more time for the things they truly enjoy. In this, the concepts of self-discipline, structure and detail are stressors for the Explorer type.

Additional stressors for an Explorer type may include: Micromanagement, regulations, routine, boredom, details, and timelines. Being that people are not one-dimensional, there are many other facets that could be uniquely frustrating to an individual. This content gives you a broad understanding of the typical stressors for each behavioral preference.

> *Don't play for safety… it's the most dangerous thing in the world ~ Hugh Walpole*

Summary of Stressors

The Explorer Type

❖ Long communication, great details, structure

❖ When others micromanage and do not allow independence

❖ When others are demanding, critical, and do not listen to creative suggestions

❖ Focusing on the regulations and tasks rather than the big picture results of the project

❖ Their tendency towards procrastination and difficulty following through with projects started.

Turn these stressors to strengths:

❖ Remind self that details are important to achieve the end result. Communicate with others by staying on topic and listening to others

❖ By following through with projects on time, greater sense of independence is fostered

❖ Recognize that others may have deadlines incorporated with each milestone. Keep a creative ideas journal. Adjust criticism so you are not taking it personally

❖ Ask yourself why the rules are in place to support the task and details of the project. Interject your own regulations to aid in the results.

I'll Have the Usual

Ahhh... The Worker disposition. People with these tendencies prefer structure, stability, and order. They thrive in situations that embrace organization. This type also lives by regulations, but there is one particular situation when they "buck the rules". This occurs when change is introduced suddenly and without detailed expression.

If you research, observe, and question individuals of various behavioral styles, you may find that Worker types cite flexibility as their greatest need for improvement. In this, being flexible when others are late, when milestones are missed, when objectives are revised, or when the highway is detoured is stressful for the Worker type. They note comfort in familiarity and along those lines, note discomfort (even pain!) with modification.

Along the same lines, just as the Explorer seeks adventure and encourages change for the sake of newness, the Worker seeks stability and bucks change, especially when merely for the sake of newness. This is one of their greatest stressors: embracing change.

If a Worker type does not strive to embrace the necessary modifications, he may become stagnant in process. For instance, if the focus is on the details of the change itself, a Worker type may not adjust to the changes in place.

As you may surmise, Worker types are no different than the other behavioral preferences in that they also have many possible stressors. Some of these additional stressors include others' inattention to detail, lack of focus, neglect of timelines, and disregard of personal follow-through. When these situations occur, a Worker type may become extremely frustrated and unable to focus on the very details they typically embrace.

Summary of Stressors

The Worker Type

❖ Personal communication, not sticking to the topic, lack of focus

❖ When others do not follow through and waste time

❖ When others do not respect formality or rules

❖ Focusing on the feelings and neglecting the specifications of the task

❖ Their inflexibility or hesitancy towards change

Turn these stressors to strengths:

❖ Remind self that others may need personal communication before presenting details in order for them to buy in to the topic

❖ Ask self: What is preventing these deadlines from being met? Getting to know the team enhances their accountability towards goals.

❖ Incorporate the team to design the rules and the consequences if those rules are broken. Some may not recognize the importance of rules.

❖ Take small changes every day so that it is not as difficult to accept larger changes when they do occur. Analyze all possibilities for better results with change.

Conclusion

Stress is the result of how we perceive a particular situation. There are two types of stress: Eustress and distress. Eustress is stress stemming from positive experiences (promotion, marriage, a new child on the way...). Distress is stress stemming from negative experiences (loss of a loved one, involuntary job change, divorce...). The stressors we mentioned for each of these behavioral styles are situations that are perceived as distressful. That is, the stressors tend to induce a negative reaction from their presence.

One of the greatest actions toward high performance is to be aware of these stressors and to follow an action plan to minimize their negative effects. Notice that it is not sufficient to know of your stressor, but it is important to take the additional step and act to reduce those stressors. The best way to do this is to face those anxieties and then to develop those qualities so that stressors actually become developed strengths.

For instance, one of my clients was discussing natural stressors that she worked into strengths. Her story is as follows: Linda is a well-respected manager in a large, prominent senior-living center. During a workshop, she noted that she is a true Navigator type and is very comfortable in that role. However, her cohorts were amazed that she was such a strong Navigator type. Each perceived Linda to be a Social Servitor because of the way she handles clients and families. Linda piped up, "I go home at night and don't want to be around people. I love making decisions. I love competition. I love achieving our goals. I dislike chatter. I dislike emotional context. I dislike touchy-feely innuendo. I love my management position, and in that, I knew I had to be good with people to be good at my job. I worked at it. Trust me, it is work!" Linda embraced those very qualities that were stressful to her: the soft skills. She is very well rounded and a highly respected leader in her community.

We can all excel in our jobs, families and relationships by facing those stressors and positively polish them into strengths. The following page has an example action-plan to develop these stressors into strengths.

The thinner the ice, the more anxious is everyone to see whether it will bear ~ Josh Billings

Stressors to Strengths: Action Plan

1. People who know me best in my professional field may think that my stressors are:

   _____

   _____

2. When I think of my current professional job, I realize my stressors are:

   _____

   _____

3. Of the above, the top three stressors that may be negatively effecting my performance most are:

   _____

   _____

4. For each of these stressors: On a daily basis I am 100% committed to the following actions to develop these stressors into strengths:

   _____

   _____

   _____

   _____

   _____

5. In accomplishing the above actions, I will reward myself by:

   _____

   _____

Stressors to Strengths:
<u>Example</u> Action Plan

1. People who know me best in my professional field may think that my stressors are: <u>I am not flexible enough, I focus too much on the task at hand, I do not listen to others. I loathe idle or informal chatter. I don't like to toy with change.</u>

2. When I think of my current professional job, I realize my stressors are: <u>No focus on the perception of others regarding the project, I may not be as flexible as needed</u>

3. Of the above, the top three stressors that may be negatively affecting my performance most are: <u>Inflexibility, lack of deeper listening, lack of focus on team.</u>

4. For each of these stressors: On a daily basis I am 100% committed to the following actions to develop these stressors into strengths: <u>Spend at least 5 minutes per team member listening to their concerns, issues, and discussion. Sit with Joe about his new ideas for project advancement. Attempt the 2 ideas discussed yesterday. Sit with the team and personally attend to the atmosphere of the team.</u>

5. In accomplishing the above actions, I will reward myself by: <u>Giving myself time to rebuild the Firebird engine. Spend as much time at home reading my book in solitude as I spend with each team member in listening.</u>

Chapter Five
Tips to Recognize the Styles in Your Project Team

The next step is to recognize these behavioral styles within your group. This chapter offers various tips to recognize these communication preferences. Some people prefer fast-paced, brief communication and others prefer slower and deliberate conversation. Recognizing communication and behavioral preferences means accurately and effectively closing deals, disseminating information, or managing projects.

One of the best means to triple the effectiveness of communication is to keep a list of those with whom you most often work. Analyze each person's communication and behavioral style. Keep a brief log of each individual's Social Compass and communication preference. Logically and realistically, we can not offer profiles like the Social Compass to everyone we meet. This chapter is meant to help recognize an individual's most preferred style without offering a profile to each person. Ask yourself: Do they tend to take charge, or are they hesitant? Are they active and confronting or thoughtful and accepting? Are they intense and controlling or calm and accommodating? Are they spontaneous or self controlled? Are they warmly outgoing or coolly reserved? Do they offer extensive detail or wish brief and logical explanation? Do they respond to words of feeling or words of logic? Each of these questions will help you recognize their preferred style. Recognizing the style may increase effective communication, morale, and productivity.

Navigator

The Navigator Style may have typical behavioral or communication patterns that can tip you off to their preference. For instance, many Navigators squirm at conversations dealing with emotional context or conversations that stray from facts and logic. As mentioned before, they may see this type of communication as a hindrance to their desired results. The Navigator style is driven by results and much of their preferred style is founded on this drive. When reviewing the questions on the previous page, the Navigator tends to take charge. They are more active and confronting. They are typically intense and controlling. Navigators desire brief and logical explanation, with great attention to fact and little mention of emotion.

Status Quo

Depending on the workplace policies, Navigator types often surround themselves with reminders of their successes. If they have an office, you may see a large "power" desk, which typically separates the Navigator type from visitors seated on the other side. You may also see trophies and other awards for their achievements. Their office or work area may have inspirational sayings or posters, most of which reflects strong leadership and success. Many times, Navigator types prefer this décor to that of photos of family and friends. Furthermore, depending on their financial status,

Navigators may seek transportation that speaks volumes of their achievements.

Tone

Typically, the tone of a Navigator exudes power and influence. When attending to their speech patterns, their voice message, their emails and memos, many will immediately recognize this type. In all of these methods, the Navigator prefers to remain in control. This may mean they talk more than listen or they state facts more than ask questions.

More formal in nature, many of their requests may sound more like commands. In this, they also prefer direct and immediate communication. For instance, when beginning a conversation, they may not say "hi" or "how are you"... they prefer to dive right into the discussion.

Pet Peeves

You may find that Navigator types become irritated when they have little sense of control. They also may become visibly frustrated when they are involved in conversation that is not brief, to the point, or bottom lined. When Navigator types become frustrated with these events, they are typically not shy to voice their discontent.

Actions

Much like their tone, their presence is also commanding. Typically, a Navigator type is very fast paced in speech and gait. They may carry a sense of hustle and bustle about them. With this commanding presence come a firm handshake and a sense of authority. The Navigator acts as if there is little time for all the day's accomplishments, but strives to reach each and every goal on the calendar.

Tips to Recognize
The Navigator Type

❖ May have a power desk separating them from visitors

❖ Visible trophies, awards, degrees

❖ Tone of authority and control

❖ Formality and power in conversation and gait

❖ May not say hi, will just dive into the conversation

❖ Firm handshake

❖ Talks more, listens less, controls the conversation

❖ States more and asks fewer questions

❖ Heightened volume and speed in intonation

❖ Dislikes not being in control

❖ Frustrated with conversation that is not brief, to the point, and bottom lined

❖ Action oriented

❖ Sense of hustle and bustle in speech and gait

❖ Speaks in terms of logic, not emotion

❖ Prefers meetings by appointment

Social Servitor

As you can imagine, the preferred communication and behavioral style of the Social Servitor is vastly different from the style of the Navigator. While the Navigator type resists discussion of feelings, of personal reflection, or of relationships, the Social Servitor thrives when these concepts are brought to their attention. Just like the Navigator, the Social Servitor has typical behavioral and communication patterns. In answering the questions in the beginning of this chapter, you may note the Social Servitor is vastly different from the Navigator. For instance, the Social Servitor is more likely to be hesitant instead of forceful. They are thoughtful and accepting. Social Servitors also tend to be calmly accommodating, with a warm, friendly nature. With this nature comes their greatest reception to words of emotion, feeling, or intuition. As you may recall, the greatest drive for the Social Servitor is the drive for belonging. This drive leads to actions and communication that considers others.

Environment

A Social Servitor's environment is one of genuine warmth. They enjoy surrounding themselves with people who have good attitudes. They design their work place to be welcoming and inviting. They typically enjoy the open door policy and, if possible, will set their space up to allow close interaction (without a power desk between them and the visitors!) Their work space may include a number of photos or reminders of family (don't be surprised to see drawings from their children).

Tone

A Social Servitor's tone is one of genuine concern. They pose more questions than they state facts, simply because they are tremendous listeners and enjoy using this strength. While the Navigator may have a louder, more commanding tone, the Social Servitor typically has a lower, quieter tone, especially when talking with strangers. This brings a great point in that Social Servitors may exhibit higher pitches, louder tone, and faster speech with those they know well.

The Social Servitor may begin conversations with a light question, for they see that as a means to get others to relax and open up to conversation. Questions may include, "How are the kids?" "How was your vacation?" "Are you feeling better?"... While other Social Servitors or Explorer types may find this to be a comfortable and friendly line of questioning, Navigators and Workers may view it as a breach of privacy or a complete waste of time. Navigators and Workers may become resentful of the inquiry. This is one reason why it may be important to recognize the behavioral and communication style before entering a discussion.

Actions

Social Servitors typically act *after* they have considered how their decision will affect the individuals involved. This thought also plays into their speech and gait. They may speak and move more thoughtfully than the Navigator types. Social Servitors have the philosophy that we need to stop and smell the roses to appreciate those who surround us.

The presence of a Social Servitor may not be as commanding as the Navigator's presence, but its effects are just as powerful. The Social Servitor focuses on harmony and cohesion. They act and invite warm conversations, open communication, and a genuine caring environment. All of this stems from their innate sense to belong.

Tips to Recognize
The Social Servitor Type

- ❖ May prefer side-by-side seating

- ❖ Workspace may include personal photos and family reminders (i.e. children's drawings)

- ❖ Slower, more deliberate gait

- ❖ Responds better to feeling words more than thought words

- ❖ Asks personal questions to ease conversation

- ❖ Concerned tone

- ❖ Lower, quieter tone, especially with strangers

- ❖ Asks more questions rather than states facts

- ❖ Natural listeners

- ❖ Invites the open-door communication policy

- ❖ Frustrated with little attention to team concern

- ❖ Dislikes disregard to their point of view/feelings

- ❖ Generally optimistic and encourages this from others

Explorer

The Explorer is, as we have discussed, a high spirited, innovative individual. The behavioral and communication tendencies for this type may be more informal than that of the Navigator or Worker and may be more expressive than that of the Social Servitor. Explorers tend to be extremely warm and outgoing. They are spontaneous in thought, speech, and action. They are very action oriented; however their actions may be more impulsive and focused on the process than the Navigators who usually focus on the end result. Explorers are also intense individuals who focus on control, specifically, wanting to do things their way. This type also attends to words of intuition or feeling more than words of detail and logic.

Stimuli

An Explorer type is driven towards physical, intellectual, emotional, or spiritual adventure. This sense of adventure sparks a connection to a stimulation of the senses. With this, the Explorer may have an office or work space that is visually stimulating. It may appear busy to visitors. It may be full of colorful adventure posters or prints. This type of space seems unorganized to most, but the Explorer has a keen sense of knowing (or at least quickly finding) where something is. To others, this busy space may impede performance but to the Explorer type, this stimulus often sparks creativity.

Excite Me

An Explorer type acts, thinks, and communicates at a very fast pace. This is similar to the Navigator type. However, it differs from the Navigator in that the Explorer often acts impulsively and communicates informally. The Navigator thinks about the big picture and bottom line within a decision and tends to communicate much more formally.

Similarly, the Explorer type speaks very quickly and bores with conversation that lacks excitement. Because of this need for excitement, they integrate stories into their expressive conversations. They may shift from one story to another, perceiving that the remote connection between stories allows for each one to be shared. In this, Explorers may also become frustrated when others seem to lag behind in the conversation. Not everyone finds it easy to connect the pertinence of each story to the topic like the Explorers do.

With this, Explorer types are also known to be expressive with their opinion. Typically, they could care less what others think of them and are more than happy to share their views. Of course, the opposite may also hold true in that Explorers appreciate honesty, even though their loud opinions may not exhibit such appreciation.

Tone

An Explorer's tone matches their high spirit. In addition to their illustrious tales, Explorers are animated in manner. They typically speak faster, louder, and with a higher pitch than the other types. They may be more apt to use vernacular in speech than do the other styles. In addition to their expressive tone, their style of communication is also open. Of the four cardinal styles, the Explorer tends to be the most informal in delivery.

They may sit closer and physically connect more frequently. A pat on the back, a jovial punch on the bicep, a hand shake and grasping of the arm may be commonplace in conversation with the Explorer.

This gregarious, active, and optimistic communication tie in to the Explorer's drive for adventure, for excitement, and in the long run, for freedom and independence.

Tips to Recognize The Explorer Type

❖ Appears unorganized to others but may be organized to themselves

❖ Visually stimulating office

❖ Busy atmosphere, full of color and adventure

❖ Like glitz and pizzazz

❖ Story tellers, no matter how it may stray from topic

❖ Informal speech: vernacular

❖ Fast speech, higher pitch and tone, louder

❖ Express opinion

❖ More contact with conversation

❖ Bores with details or slow conversations

❖ Frustrated with micromanagement and step by step direction

❖ Speaks in terms of intuition and impulse not necessarily detail or logic

Worker

The Worker's style is distinctly different from the Explorer's style. When comparing the two, it is fairly easy to see the dissimilarities. For instance, the Worker type is coolly reserved whereas the Explorer is warm and outgoing. The Worker type is more deliberate and thoughtful than the Explorer. They tend to think in terms of logic, expecting detailed and structured explanation. Worker types may think through every angle before acting, and the Explorer types may act first, often impulsively.

It's All in the Details

Whether looking at workspace, emails, or voice messages, it's all in the details for a Worker type. The Worker's office space may appear to be extremely organized. This does not mean it is free of piles, but if there are piles in the office, those piles are well organized. Typically, their space may have the least amount of personal items, but when décor is considered, more than likely, simple, clean cut, and specific items adorn the space.

With emails and voice messages, you will find that Workers tend to send and desire to receive very detailed messages. They need to know the step-by-step action plan and offer this information when leaving messages as well. What one person may write in a two paragraph email, a Worker may write in a two page email.

Tone

A Worker's tone is much more reserved and low key than an Explorer's tone. Workers tend to speak quieter, in a lower pitch, and at a more deliberate pace. They would rather digest all of the options before making a decision. This is also true in conversation. Workers would rather sit back and listen, deliberately choosing their response and reactions in a meeting. With this, their conversation is focused and they frustrate easily with stories or other methods that may appear to deviate from the topic.

Because of the desire to think before acting, the Worker prefers written conversation, as it allows the information to be read, reread, and digested before responding This tone carries into their gait as well, as the Worker type tends to move in a more deliberate and measured manner.

Communication

Communication with a Worker is more formal in nature. There is little room for vernacular or jovial gestures. The Worker prefers scheduled visits that address the details and are driven by the guidelines. In this, Worker types also ask many questions to clarify specifics. They think of the options and consequences to each detail before moving onto the next topic of discussion.

Conversations are fact- and task-oriented, with little attention paid to the emotional or personal issues that team members may face. They respond best to words of thought and logic, and shy from personal stories or emotional context.

When meeting with a Worker type, it may be very apparent that the personal space is more emphasized than it is with an Explorer type. Worker types prefer more space between themselves and others. They may have an office that is symmetrically divided, with plenty of space between their chairs and the chairs of others.

While Explorer types may see the Worker style as aloof, rigid, and dry, those who know Worker types may get to see a side of them that includes humor, loyalty, and creativity. This type does prefer all of the details before making decisions. Their desire for structure and perfection feeds into their need for specifics.

Tips to Recognize
The Worker Type

❖ May have organized office space... Even the paper piles appear organized!

❖ Clean cut appearance: dress, emails, and letters

❖ Ask questions for details

❖ Prefer the formality of distance

❖ Concrete or task oriented in conversation

❖ Driven by guidelines

❖ Prefers "thought" words, logic and facts

❖ Frustrated when asked to share their feelings

❖ Prefer focused and on-topic conversations

❖ Would choose written vs. oral communication

❖ Slower, deliberate, measured movement and responses

❖ Frustrated when timelines, guidelines, and details are ignored

The Four Cardinal Styles: A Story

Four members of your management team were asked to contact each of their team members about the upcoming company picnic. Each of these four members has very different behavioral and communication styles. This is how they responded:

<u>Nathan</u>

Nathan chose to respond by email, since he could connect to each member with a few simple strokes. This would save time and complete the task effectively AND efficiently. This is Nathan's email:

"Please find below the date, time and directions for the company picnic. If you have any questions, please address them to Adrienne, my assistant."

It appears that Nathan is a Navigator. The message is brief, bright, and delivered to everyone at once. It explains the big picture. Any questions in detail would be addressed to someone other than Nathan!

> *It is my ambition to say in ten sentences what others say in a whole book. ~ Nietzsche*

<u>Sophie</u>

Sophie had a team meeting with cookies, chips, bottled water, and soda. She beamed as she looked at her team.

"I have an announcement," she said with a quiet excitement, *"our company picnic is coming up and I wanted to make sure each of you is*

personally invited! I would love to see you and your families attend. I am also heading the pot-luck committee and would like to know what each of you can bring, and if you are able to come. If there is anything I can do to make it easier for you to attend let me know and hopefully, we can work something out..."

Of course, Sophie continued to visit with each person, gathering their choice of dish to bring and reminiscing over last year's event. She explained location, date and time to each individual. She loves the company picnic!

It appears that Sophie is a Social Servitor. The message is personal and yet team oriented. It explains the big picture and offers some detail. She is involved personally and professionally.

Evan

Evan decided to discuss the picnic at the next team meeting. He sauntered into the conference room, gave Joe a big pat on the back and sat in his chair.

"Hey guys! How's it goin'? Yeah, we actually have something fun today. Hey, the company picnic is coming up. I left the flyers in my office, but I'll get them to you in your boxes... Ok, ok... to be certain you will get them... Jeannie, would you mind getting them out to everyone? Great." Someone in the group mentioned something listed on the agenda. *"Oh, yeah, we didn't get to that last week. Is it still something we need to go over?..."* And the meeting took off in another direction, although Evan's intention was to cover the potluck and other aspects of the picnic.

From the sound of Evan's boisterous tone and informal approach with his group, Evan appears to prefer the Explorer style. He had great intentions to cover all of the details of the picnic, but his focus easily swerved onto another topic. Details, shmetails!

Wilma

Wilma had spent the last forty-five minutes devising a two-page email to send to her group. After reviewing what she had written, she decided to include most of that information as an attachment.

Her email read as follows,

"*Dear Group,*

As is customary each year at this time, our company picnic is upon us. I was asked to contact each of you in regards to the location, time, date and events that will transpire on that day. I have attached last year's itinerary, and being that our committee has approved it for this year, it will also stand for this year's events.

The picnic is in one month, on Saturday, June 8. The picnic will be at Ponderosa Park, in Pavilions 4, 5, 6 and 7. Your children and spouses are welcome to join. The pool will be available, so bring your swimming gear.

The picnic is primarily funded by the efforts of the Human Resources Community Outreach team. They have generously donated their time and efforts in fundraising and drawings to fund most of the events. It is still necessary that each of the attendees bring a side dish. A potluck list is available in the break room. You may review it during lunch hours or breaks..."

The email goes on.

From the extensive detail of this email (and it is only a partial view), it appears that Wilma is a Worker. She painstakingly reviewed her options to offer the information. She chose a detailed and written format. This information appears to be more formal in nature, as is typical of the Worker.

Conclusion

Each cardinal style has preferred means of acting, responding, and communicating. Neither of these options is right or wrong, they are just different! As a manager or team leader, being able to match your communication style to the style of your team member can positively impact results, behavior, and performance. In order to adjust to your team member's more preferred style, one must be able to recognize these styles. This chapter discussed tips to help with this recognition. The next chapter will discuss how to adjust to the communication styles of those with whom you work.

> *No person was ever honored for what he received. Honor has been the reward for what he gave ~ Calvin Coolidge*

Chapter Six
So What!... Now What?
(Adapting for Excellence)

There is much more to a person's behavior than personality. As we have discussed, one's perception also plays a role in how he will act. So, how do perceptions form? Much of this can be traced back to experiences, as well as the biological makeup of an individual. Can we change our past experiences or genetic disposition? No. Can we change our perceptions of these things and of things to come? Yes. Do we want to change? This depends!

If you address someone who thinks and acts similarly to the way you think and act, you may not feel pressed to change communication styles. However, if you address someone who may be your opposite, altering your methods of communication is a winning strategy. Why? If the delivery of the message is not the listener's natural style, the listener will tune out and not hear the message! This means it is likely that a key piece of the message was not heard at all. This can have a profoundly negative impact on the project's development. Most project managers and team leaders cite this is cause for their greatest difficulties (and later realize it just needed a simple adjustment to prevent this!)

> *Speech is power: speech is to persuade, to convert, to compel ~ Ralph Waldo Emerson*

The point of this book is to introduce you to various behavioral and communication styles. It is not to diagnose or treat any type of personality disorders or mental health issues. As we've mentioned over and over, people are not one dimensional. The purpose of this chapter is to look at the dimension regarding communication preferences. While we may not need to understand why people behave, think, or act they way they do, we do need to at least recognize their preferred communication and behavioral style. Seeing the communication piece of the complete picture can aid in performance, morale, and results. With limited time to interact on deeper levels, the quickest means to spur results and build more effective communication in the workplace is to recognize and adapt to your team's communication and behavioral preferences.

Why Do I Have To Be The One To Adjust?

There are numerous research studies that explore the benefits and success ratios of people who are able to adapt and leverage. Most people who have the knowledge (like that given in this book) and act on that knowledge are more likely to reach higher planes of success than those who do not act on that knowledge (or may not know!) It is up to you to take this information and put it to use. Most managers and leaders find that implementing this information reduces miscommunication, poor work performance, and lower levels of morale. They find that others are interested in their ability to adapt and are able to train these concepts to their team.

Those who choose not to act on this information are doing what they have always done... More than likely, they are getting what they have always gotten. If they want more, if they want to break through the glass ceiling, if they want to excel beyond their typical levels of achievement, changes need to be made. For the purposes of this chapter, changes include adapting your communication style to those styles of your team.

Can We Adapt?

Many scientists, psychologists, and sociologists will tell you that one of the greatest powers of humankind is the power to adapt. It is a great sign of intelligence, when beings can adjust to their environment. So, can we adapt our communication or behavioral styles to mirror the styles of others? Absolutely. Humans are highly intelligent beings. We have amazed ourselves at our own progress. Adjusting communication styles seems like a small task in comparison to some of the other wondrous feats we have accomplished.

Recall I mentioned that personalities seem to remain fixed over time. This book is not one of personalities, but of behavioral and communication preferences (which have ties to our personalities). We can adapt our actions, our reactions, our communication styles or our negative or positive thoughts. When we adjust, we temporarily meet the needs of others in order to meet our needs. This reminds me of the age-old study of the chimpanzees and the ant hill. One chimp in particular was determined to eat the ants that were burrowing deeply within a tree trunk. He started licking the tree where the ants were entering and exiting, trying to catch as many ants as possible. Did this work? Sure. Was it efficient? No. So, his brow deep in thought, he tried to stick his finger in the tree's hollow. His fingers were too big. After a moment, he looked around and found a stick, still sticky with the sweet tree resin. He stuck the stick in the ant's hollowed tree and the ants climbed all over the stick. He pulled the stick out of the tree and licked the ants off the stick. He did this over and over... Finally, he was able to efficiently and effectively eat the ants. He adapted. The stick was no longer a stick. It became an eating utensil.

So, what does this story have to do with human being's adaptation? Well, the chimp was able to eat some ants by licking the tree where the ants were. It worked but it was not as efficient as it could have been. Our communication methods work, but are they always effective or efficient? NO! This is why so many leaders and project managers cite that they probably spend more than 30% of their time correcting issues stemming from miscommunication.

Also recall that when we adjust, we are temporarily meeting the needs of others in order to meet our needs. The tree hole was too small for anything but the stick, so to meet that, the chimp had to use the stick in order to reach the ants. The stick met the needs of the ants with resin and food. The chimp was able to adapt in order to meet his needs: eating ants! If a chimp can adapt, people certainly can adapt. The question now is: Will you?

Not being able to control events, I control myself; and I adapt myself to them, if they do not adapt themselves to me
~ Michel de Montaigne

Adjusting/Adapting

Now that we know we can adapt, and we recognize why we want to adjust, the next step is to learn some simple tips to modify our style to match that of each of our team members. These tips are time tested, results-oriented methods. Among the different personality, behavioral, and communication profiles and trainings, these tips have helped tens of millions of people excel and succeed at work and in their relationships. The titles used for each style may differ among various trainings and profiles, but (for the most part) the tips to recognize and to adapt to each style are universal. Being results-oriented, I want you to have these simple tips so that you can experience positive results as well! These are the very tips discussed in this chapter.

Navigator Style

Those who may prefer the Navigator style of communication live by FDR's famous quote: "Be sincere, be brief, be seated." They opt for communication to be logical and to the point. For these types, you want to bottom-line it first and foremost. Plan on visiting with those who prefer the Navigator style as if you only had two minutes to get your point across. Now, what is important to remember, is that Navigators usually prefer scheduled appointments for a face to face or phone conversation. After you schedule this appointment, use these tips in your discussion.

The Navigator style sways towards succinct presentations, including visual graphs and agenda. You want to show them what's in it for them. Being competitive, they need to know the value of this communication and how it can help enhance the results of the project. This is not only true of the face to face communication, but also virtual communication. When writing letters, memos, or emails, be very distinct in your message. If you need to meet with them again to clarify something, close by noting just that.

When communicating with one who naturally tends toward the Navigator style, it is important that you allow that person to control the conversation. How do you do this? Use soft-close questions. Questions like: What do you think? Hasn't this been the problem? Where do you want this project to go? What other ideas do you have? Don't you agree? (knowing they do). By offering them questions that allow them to think along your lines, to agree with your topic, and to believe they had a strong influence in the idea, those with Navigator styles may be more apt to buy into the conversation.

As you spend time with the Navigator style, recognize their pace of communication. Match it. If they are speaking quickly, then increase your rate of speech. If they are using short, bright sentences then you use the same. Show them your reasoning and logic behind the topic. When you introduce your point of view, make sure you have done your research and use facts (not feelings or emotional content) to support your message.

If they are using words like "think", "see", "results", "vision", use these same words (and other words they use) in your discussion. You want them to feel comfortable. You want them to attend to the message, not the delivery of the message. You want to speak their language. You want to get your point across, and get it across effectively and efficiently!

When you give feedback to those who sway towards the Navigator style, you want to make sure it is behind closed doors (and don't surprise them!) Be brief, focus on the issue and not on the personal connection. Be honest and base the feedback on facts. Because of their competitive nature and need to see results, it is important to work with Navigator types to structure a way to improve. Give them the reigns and sense of control over their need for action. With this, it is also essential to provide Navigators with a big picture of what is expected and how they may have fallen short. Once they are on board and have a sense of control, they will work hard to make the improvements and to be the best.

Offering compliments is the same model as offering feedback. You want to be brief and specific. Compliment them on their leadership abilities, on their results, and on how it has helped to reach the big picture. Try not to use feeling words or emotional compliments, for these are not the specifics that spark a Navigator style.

Those of the Navigator preference will also tell you they like to be complimented and rewarded with tokens of achievement, from things like blue ribbons to trophies to gift certificates to executive gifts (and of course, including monetary bonuses!). Feed into their sense of results, their competitive nature, and their desire to excel, and you should have a strong means to motivate, compliment, and reward those of the Navigator preference.

Leadership: The art of getting someone else to do something you want done because he wants to do it ~ Dwight D. Eisenhower

---

Adapting to the Navigator Style

❖ Be sincere, be brief, be seated.

❖ Use terms of logic. Bottom line it!

❖ Succinct presentations with graphs and agenda.

❖ Show them what's in it for them.

❖ What is the value of the communication? How can it help the results of the project?

❖ Allow them to control the conversation. Use questions to get their input and encourage their conversation.

❖ Match their pace and tone of communication. If they speak quickly, increase your speed. If they use shorter, more logical sentences, then you do the same.

❖ Use their vocabulary. Implement their terms. Many of these terms are: think, vision, results, bottom-line, action, big-picture, deadlines...

❖ Focus feedback on the project. Be honest and succinct. Use facts.

❖ Get their input and buy-in to action plans that correct the issues.

❖ Compliment with rewards of achievement

❖ Recognize their leadership abilities, and their push towards results.

❖ Feed into their sense of competition and excellence.

Social Servitor Style

Those who tend towards the style of the Social Servitor prefer a much different delivery of communication than the Navigator style. For instance, with the Navigator, you want to be brief and logical. With the Social Servitor, you want a longer, warmer, and more connected communication delivery. Two minutes to a Social Servitor is just the beginning of a warm communication, full of personal interaction and team connection. When you are preparing to speak with a Social Servitor, be prepared to spend more time with them. This style also is very receptive to the open door policy, where no appointment is necessary.

Along these regards, the Social Servitor prefers face to face communication over virtual communication. This is not to say they will not email or send memos, but if you truly want them to listen, understand, and buy into your conversation, be certain to meet them in a warm environment conducive to cohesion. Asking for a meeting to take place in an area full of noisy phones, constant disruption, or of little comfort may be asking for failure. Taking them out to coffee, meeting in a quiet and cozy office, or connecting near the bench outdoors may be a perfect place to share ideas.

Additionally, you want to mirror the communication style of the Social Servitor just as you would the Navigator style. If the Social Servitor asks how you are, reply and follow suit. If they speak a little slower than you naturally do, be certain to slow your pace.

Be certain to note the wording they choose. Typically, they hear and speak in terms of "feeling", "we", "us", "team", and "harmony". When you emphasize these terms, you will be on the same page as they are, which makes it easier for them to clearly receive the message as you intend.

People who naturally prefer this style also are very sensitive to the needs of others. When working with a Social Servitor, be prepared to talk more than listen, as they naturally ask questions and listen to your input. However, along these same lines, they may be very eager to interject their stories. They want to be certain that the two of you connect, so they will try to connect in stories, thoughts, and ideas. This is also something they expect from others, so be prepared to share something to strengthen that connection.

When communicating with a Social Servitor, you can offer a big picture and some detail, as they can see a bit of both. What they are really interested in is how the big picture and the details will affect their team and the individuals involved. By focusing on the connection, cohesion, and community, you are apt to get the Social Servitors on board.

When you have questions of a Social Servitor, tactfully ask for clarification, as they tend to avoid conflict. Explain why the clarification is needed, placing blame on no one. Focus strictly on the questions for clarification and emphasize how the answers to these questions will lead to success.

Just as the Social Servitors are sensitive to other's needs, they also are sensitive to their own needs. This must be considered when offering feedback. The biggest need for the Social Servitor is to belong. Depending on how feedback is given, a Social Servitor may perceive criticism as something that actually tears them from the team instead of connecting them to the team. From this, those who prefer the Social Servitor style typically take feedback more personally than might the Navigator or Explorer styles. So, in order to get the message across and still maintain harmony, it is important to focus on the project and refrain from using words that may seem as if it is a personal attack. What I suggest using are I-Statements. Use the model: "I feel (remember, you are dealing with a feeling type) _____ (disappointed, upset, anxious...) because _____ (the project was past deadline or the project did not meet expectations...). As you can see, the word "you" is nowhere in this line of communication. The minute you use "you" with criticism, people often put up a wall because they feel you are attacking them personally and not criticizing the work. Compare these: "I feel frustrated because the task was not as thoroughly completed as we've discussed. Let's work on improving this." to "This job is not up to expectations. You did not complete it as we've discussed in the past. You need to return to the notes and improve it." The second statement may cause frustration, anxiety, and even anger if spoken to a Social Servitor or Worker. The first statement may be more appropriate in motivating change and preventing discord. This is not only true for the Social Servitor style, but also for the Worker style.

Complimenting the Social Servitor is a bit different than offering feedback. When complimenting, be certain to address how their personal contributions added to the success of the task. Unlike the Navigator style, the Social Servitor style prefers feeling words and emotional compliments. They desire to be recognized for their contributions to the team and the task. They do not necessarily desire the ribbons or trophies that Navigator types may yearn, but they do seek honest, quiet, and sincere recognition that their work means something to the team. Many people of the Social Servitor preference embrace rewards that deal with supporting others, supporting their creative outlets, and providing a cooperative group with which to work. These are great rewards for a Social Servitor.

> *Sweet is the scene where genial friendship plays*
> *The pleasing game of interchanging praise*
> *~ Oliver Wendell Holmes*

By using these tips when working with those who prefer the Social Servitor style, you may find they buy into the topic, project, or conversation. When they buy into what you are saying, they are more likely to closely attend and perceive the message or actions as was meant to be perceived. Effective and efficient communication will improve results, as well as the team's morale. Enhancing team morale is a common goal of Social Servitors. Enhancing results is a common goal of Navigators. While both are very different in natural communication style, they are not uncomplimentary. While satisfying one's goal, the other's is achieved as well.

Adapting to the Social Servitor Style

❖ Be warm, be open, be connected.

❖ Use terms of personal interaction and team connection.

❖ Prefers face to face over virtual communication.

❖ Meet in a comfortable, warm, friendly environment.

❖ Be prepared to listen and talk. They do listen well, but also want to be listened to when they have input.

❖ Match their pace and tone of communication. If they speak more deliberately, then slow down to match that speed.

❖ Use their vocabulary. Implement their terms. Many of these terms are: we, us, team, feelings, emotion, harmony, cohesion, and process.

❖ Ask for clarification with any questions, allowing them to offer input without fear of conflict.

❖ Focus feedback on the project. Be honest, sensitive and diplomatic. Use I-Statements.

❖ Recognize their personal contributions to the team and efforts.

❖ Reward with cooperative group effort, verbal and public (although not too public) recognition.

Explorer Style

The Explorer style of communication is much more relaxed and spirited than that of the Navigator or Worker styles. The Explorers opt for communication to be quick, to be enthusiastic, to be informal, and to be creative. For this type of communication, you want to invite (and listen to) their creative ideas and options. They want to be heard, want to explore innovative solutions, and want to act.

When meeting with one who prefers the Explorer style, be certain to meet in a more informal setting. Also, sit near her. Sitting away from her may just give her enough distance to daydream. Recall the Explorer types may firmly shake your hand, give you a jolly slap on the back, or sit next to you with their feet on the coffee table. They are very comfortable with this setting and actually listen and discuss best in this type of environment.

The Explorer prefers presentations that discuss many options and opportunities. Because of their multi-topic thought process, they prefer meetings that incorporate several learning modalities (visual, audio, kinesthetic...). With each of these modalities, it is important to ask for (and validate) their opinion and ideas. In doing so, you may make the conversation very comfortable for them. This also enhances their interest in the conversation. If you know Explorer types, you know that keeping them interested is important if you want them to truly listen!

As you communicate with one who prefers the Explorer style, match their speed and course of conversation. You will notice they naturally speak quickly (and may get frustrated with those who do not). Because of their quick thought and speech, they tend to jump from topic to topic. Others may find this multi-thought conversation to be rather chaotic and frustrating, but the Explorer type finds this a natural means to sort through all the possibilities and brainstorm with others. This knowledge is valuable, as adapting to this speed of conversation and multi-thought processing will win the attention of the Explorer.

> *Creation is a drug I can't do without ~ Cecil B. DeMille*

Furthermore, Explorer types may perk up when conversations include terms like "new", "innovative", "fun", and "independent". Now, I realize these terms are not always appropriate (auditing taxes may not be fun for many folks), but when they are appropriate, use them! More terms that spark an interest in Explorers are those that relate to the process, the beginning of the project, and the people involved. If you overload conversation with details or logic, an Explorer may daydream and miss the message.

Because of their love for creativity and new ideas, it is important to listen as well as ask questions to keep Explorers on target. Ask them what their ideas are. Ask them how the idea will be implemented. Ask them when it will be completed. This way, those great ideas are brought into reality. Additionally, these questions can control the focus and time of the conversation. This is important as the Explorer does not necessarily heed the clock or stay on one task at a time.

Along the same lines of focus, Explorer types appreciate stories within conversation. Be prepared to attach a story to the theme, for they will probably do the same. In fact, they may tell three or four stories they feel are related (but many others may not clearly see the connection!) By asking questions (what, when, how...), you are able to control the conversation, get their input, hear their ideas, and see direction.

The Explorer styles have honestly noted that they bore easily, especially with detailed conversation. In order to assure that they've received the message clearly (and attended to the content), it is a great idea to ask for them to summarize what they heard and the action steps they will take. In fact, this is something I teach anyone who manages or coaches others. It increases optimal communication and decreases misunderstandings and rumors. It is also an opportunity to be involved in the conversation and to know their ideas were heeded.

When feedback is given to an Explorer type, make sure that it is honest. They typically respect honesty, but may need to have some time to explore the issue (brainstorming creative and plausible solutions is a wonderful step in feedback). Furthermore, much of the feedback may focus on the lack of self-discipline and project completion. Get their ideas on how to correct this and hold them accountable.

When complimenting an Explorer, place them in the lime light. They enjoy the public recognition and center of attention. Additionally, make sure the compliment is honest, genuine, and deserved. Focus on their creativity, their enthusiasm, and their impact on the team project.

> *The average man does not get pleasure out of an idea because he thinks it is true; he thinks it is true because he gets pleasure out of it ~ H. L. Mencken*

Adapting to the Explorer Style

❖ Be relaxed, informal, and creative.

❖ Use terms of innovation, fun, and spirit.

❖ Present the multiple options and opportunities. Use multi-learning modalities (visual, oral, kinesthetic) in meetings.

❖ Ask for their ideas and brainstorm how they would work.

❖ Ask them questions to keep them on track and make ideas realistic: What, How, When?

❖ Use stories in conversation. Allow them to interject and join in the discussion.

❖ Match their pace and tone of communication. If they speak quickly, increase your speed. Connect multiple topics in one discussion.

❖ Use their vocabulary. Implement their terms. Many of these terms are: innovative, fun, independent, process, start up, challenge...

❖ They bore easily, so ask them to summarize the conversation and clarify the action steps.

❖ Be honest with feedback. Get their input and buy-in to action plans that correct the issues, allow for creative solutions to the problems.

❖ Compliment them in the lime light. Put them in the center of attention (when deserved!).

❖ Honestly recognize their creativity, enthusiasm and impact on the team project.

Worker Style

Those who naturally sway towards the Worker style of communication live by the saying, "It's all in the details". Like the Navigator preference, the Worker prefers logic and intelligent conversation. Different from the Navigator style is the Worker's attention to detail. When you are preparing to visit with the Worker style, you may want to make sure you initiate a meeting request in written and oral form. In order for those of the Worker style to dot their i's and cross their t's, they may also prefer a summary of the conversation to be in written form. When meeting with an individual of the Worker style, plan on using both written and oral communication, on confirming the appointment, and on either asking them for or sending to them a summary and action plan after the meeting.

The Worker style prefers presentations full of details, research, and concrete evidence. Plan on visiting with them for a longer period of time than you would the Navigator style. The Worker may have plenty of questions regarding the specifications of the topic and they expect those questions to be answered. Therefore, the presentation itself should be loaded with data, graphs (if applicable), testimonials, research results, and more! Giving them handouts or a binder with this information is important, as they typically will not immediately come to a decision. They tend to think about the conversation and digest it. After sorting through the options and evidence, they will come to an analytical and measured decision.

The Worker preference also tends toward more formal means of communication than that of the Explorer or Social Servitor preferences. This means they wish to be addressed by their title (Mr., Ms., Dr...) until they get to know you. In this, they will also address you in the same manner.

Along those lines of formality, the Worker style also prefers a more structured environment. Asking them to lunch or coffee for a meeting is not a good idea, for they would rather talk shop at the shop! Meeting in an office, conference room, or other space away from distraction is the best selection for a meeting. They prefer some distance in seating at the meeting, unlike the Explorer styles who enjoy sitting next to someone.

In connection to this desire for formality is the preference for conversations that are logical, detailed and without personal context. They sway towards words like: "think", "research", "details", "evidence" and "disciplined". When you speak with a Worker, match your terminology with those used by the Worker type.

You also want to match the rate of speech to that of the Worker style. They tend to speak in a much more deliberate rate, as they think before responding. They are easily frustrated by the natural speech of the Explorer (fast, multiple-track, and seemingly disorganized). Needless to say, the Explorer may become frustrated by the Worker style (deliberate, one-track, detailed, and extremely structured). So, when speaking to any of these styles, be certain to match speed, track, terminology, and formality. By doing so, you win the attention and direction of that person.

When giving feedback to a Worker type, you want to make certain it is behind closed doors (this is actually sound advice for any type). As we mentioned with the Social Servitors, use

I-statements, as the Worker style tends to take criticism more personally, since they put much effort into the task at hand. Furthermore, you want to structure the conversation by focusing on the details and facts, not on personal feelings about issues. They typically could care less about how you "feel", but will lay much validity into what is concrete, and may do whatever it takes to better those results.

> *Get the facts or the facts will get you. And when you get 'em, get 'em right, or they will get you wrong. ~ Thomas Fuller*

Offering compliments to a Worker style is also an art form. Unlike many of the other preferences, those who sway towards the Worker style would rather get their compliments and rewards in private. The ultimate reward is knowing that all of their hard work led to perfect results and success. With this, they are typically not receptive to public honors or being in the lime light. They want others to know that the results were possible because of their hard work, dedication, and attention to the specifics. One of the biggest frustrations for those with the Worker style is to have someone else take recognition for their work. Let the Worker know his job is greatly appreciated, that his attention to detail is important to the team and the task, and that he has earned the great reward of additional responsibilities or projects (they love more work!) The Worker style tends toward a more quiet recognition (based on facts), but does like the honest recognition nonetheless.

Adapting to the Worker Style

❖ Focus on the facts. Use concrete evidence.

❖ Use terms of logic. Supply plenty of details.

❖ Succinct presentations with graphs, research, and structured outlines.

❖ Allow time to think prior to asking for a decision.

❖ Focus on formalities. Meet in a quiet work setting, not usually at lunch or over coffee.

❖ Set seating at a distance, not close seating like with the Explorer style.

❖ Match their pace and tone of communication. If they speak more deliberately, then think and respond more deliberately.

❖ Use their vocabulary. Implement their terms. Many of these terms are: think, logic, details, proof, do it right, results, structure, focus.

❖ Focus feedback on the project. Be honest and succinct. Use facts. Use I-Statements.

❖ Get their input and buy-in to action plans that correct the issues. How can it be better?

❖ Compliment in private with genuine gratitude for their hard work, dedication, and attention to details.

❖ Let them know their job is important, how well they have impacted the team, and give them more projects and responsibilities as a reward.

Proven Directions in Leadership

By adapting your style as a proven leader, a project manager, a team member, or a promising supervisor, you will find that you are able to get more accomplished with your time. You may also find that your stakeholders and C-level project participants appreciate the conversations and may hold your project in higher regards, compared to someone who may not speak in the same style and who annoys, frustrates, or intimidates them.

A healthy and effective leader will be able to adjust style as called by the situation. Those leaders who refuse to bend often break in terms of leadership loyalty, productivity, or morale. Not all great leaders adapt and not all poor leaders refuse to adapt, but when looking at the big picture and most common situations, it appears that those who can adjust have greater 360 feedback scores, greater employee morale, greater team productivity, and fewer communication problems.

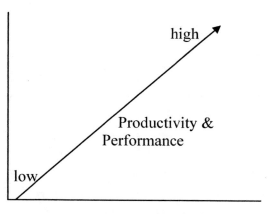

This figure exemplifies leadership performance and productivity. If a leader is not either sensitive or controlling, or either people- or project-oriented, performance will be extremely low. More than likely, this leader is unskilled and unmotivated in the position.

When a leader has the ability to control, to be sensitive, to focus on both the project and the people, performance and productivity is high. When a manager is only controlling and project oriented OR only sensitive and people oriented, performance and productivity will be minimal.

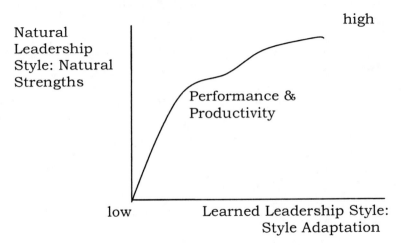

Natural
Leadership
Style: Natural
Strengths

high

Performance &
Productivity

low

Learned Leadership Style:
Style Adaptation

When a team leader or project manager is able to adapt and pool from natural strengths and learned strengths, performance and productivity is optimal. When a team leader or project manager is not able to adapt and uses only those natural strengths, performance and productivity is far from optimal. When people can (and do) adapt readily, they report less stress and greater satisfaction at work and at home.

Conclusion

These tips can truly help to decrease the number of problems stemming from poor communication, IF you use them! The question is: will you implement these tips? You have probably been fairly successful speaking to others in your "language". How much more effective and efficient could your job be if you were able to practice these tips and speak in a language others understand?

The time to practice these tips is when it seems least crucial. These are the times when it is easier to form habits. For instance, if you are going on a diet, do you start your diet around the holidays, trying to be perfect? Some people do, and they succeed. Most people who start a diet during the holidays say they fail miserably. Why? Because those habits are not formed, and they try to practice these unformed habits when it is most necessary (and most difficult). The same holds true for communication. While it may never seem like a quiet time to practice, you will find more opportunities to practice these tips than you realize. Practice with family. Practice at work. I say, practice with a pet! "Today, puppy, you are a Navigator and I am only going to talk to you in Navigator style. Tomorrow, you will be a Worker!"

Research indicates it takes about six weeks to form a good habit. Practice (this is action) these tips day in and day out for six weeks. Attend to any signs of heightened results or morale. See for yourself how well this adaptation works!

> *Sow an act and you reap a habit,*
> *Sow a habit and you reap a character,*
> *Sow a character and you reap a destiny.* ~ *Charles Reade*

Chapter Seven
People and Workplace Problems

Problems in the workplace are inevitable. When you get more than one person in a room, eventually, there will be difference of opinion, conflict, or misunderstanding. Ben Franklin captured this thought in his saying, "Three may keep a secret if two of them are dead." Since we can't (and more likely, choose not to) live in a bubble, all alone with no personal interaction whatsoever, it is important to recognize how to deal with others so that these problems are minimized.

As we have noted, people are different, unique, and definitely dynamic. Even if people think alike, experiences and genetics dictate that we may perceive situations differently. This may lead to some issues at home, at work, or in the social setting. This chapter will focus on some of the most common issues within the workplace (you may find that some of these problems transcend into the home or social settings). In addition, this chapter will look at some of the best ways to prevent these problems (or at least address them if they are already present).

Conflict

One of the biggest issues within the work site is conflict. Why? Different situations spur conflict for different people. People have different definitions for conflict. People react differently to conflict. It is everywhere, and it is fueled by the differences among us.

According to the Random House Dictionary, conflict means to oppose or clash. It is a battle or an antagonism. We see people clash daily, and often this clash leads to a performance crash! While some people may thrive and perform well with heated and energetic discussions, others may sink or perform poorly by the distraction of what they believe to be arguments and battles. It's all about one's experience and perception, laid in the foundation of personality and genetics.

One of the better activities I use in workshops relates to the difference in opinion to conflict. I often split workshop participants into groups. Sometimes these groups are in accordance to their most preferred style (Navigator, Social Servitor, Explorer, Worker) and other times it is in accordance to other factors (job description, age...) Once the groups are formed, I ask each group to come up with the definition of conflict. I then ask them to brainstorm positive and negative aspects of conflict. I may also have them discuss consequences to conflict, as well as name some situations (as a group) that they consider to encourage conflict.

The different group responses are amazing. It is a powerful activity in that each group can see what the other groups consider to represent conflict, and what conflict means to them. Each group has a different outlook and what one group may consider to be trivial, another group may consider to be a "big deal." After hearing the difference of opinions, experiences, and reactions, individuals come to a realization that, by golly, we are different! We embrace different strengths and shy from different situations. An even greater step is to not only understand that we are different, but also to appreciate the differences within each group. This is important to consider when working with others, as a project manager or team leader.

So, what begets conflict? Rumors, miscommunication, differences, perceptions, experiences, personalities, and resentment all stir up conflict. When rumors and miscommunication occur, people often become defensive. We are on the war path. We are in battle (another term for conflict). We look for conflict.

Our differences in experience, personality, genetics, health, religion and professional roles also play a part in conflict. People may not understand these differences. This unfamiliarity is a fancy fuel for conflict. We ignore, despise, study, or fight that which we do not understand. Most of these will lead to conflict, as we may be in opposition to or clash with whatever it is that we do not understand.

All of these things lead to our perceptions. What do we perceive the other person is doing? If we perceive them to be egging us on, we will react accordingly. If we perceive them to be venting with us because they just received horrible news from home, we react accordingly. Here is an example of conflict, founded on perceptions:

Jane began her new job. She did not know anyone else in her department, and no one else stopped in to get to know her. The others thought she was aloof, uncaring, and even snobby. She thought the others were unfriendly, clique-ish, and difficult to talk to.

One day, Jane was attending to the phones that were constantly ringing. Just then, some clients approached Jane's counter. Her back was to them as she was searching through files and talking to someone on the phone. At that time, one of her co-workers came over and saw the clients patiently waiting. He gave Jane a dirty look and attended to the clients.

Jane was flustered. She was so busy answering the phones; she had not noticed the clients standing there.

In this situation, the conflict is just beginning. There are two different perceptions brewing. One is the co-worker's perception that Jane is just chatting on the phone and not attending to others. "What right does she have? All she does is hide and talk on the phone. She better get to work!" She is aloof, uncaring, and snobby to the others.

Jane's perception is that she was busy attending to the client on the phone and had not noticed the two clients who were waiting at the counter. She was busy, energetic, and helpful. After she received the dirty look from her co-worker, she became flustered, frustrated, and even angry. "What right does he have? I only have two hands, two ears, and two eyes! He's so lazy... why doesn't **he** help? I'm **not** the only one working."

Two perceptions. One environment. Two reactions: neither of them is healthy or accurate! Is conflict on its way? If neither of these individuals tries to understand the other person, then conflict is on its way. Could this conflict be avoided? Absolutely. Might this situation impede high performance for these two characters? Sure.

> *He who does not understand your silence will probably not understand your words ~ Elbert Hubbard*

Styles and Conflict

Needless to say, when people of different communication preferences get together, conflict festers. For instance, those Navigator styles may speak in big picture, with great emphasis on the project and results. The Social Servitor style may become frustrated by the Navigator's lack of attention to people or feelings. The Worker style may become frustrated by the Navigator's lack of attention to details. The Explorer style may become frustrated by the Navigator's competitive nature and aggressive commands to finish on time. The Navigator style may become frustrated with the Social Servitor's desire to chat, with the Worker's deliberate pace, or with the Explorer's flighty story-telling.

When it comes to different communication styles, there are many things that may spark conflict and work place problems. Each of the more common aspects of these issues is discussed below.

Navigator Style

The Navigator is typically a no-nonsense communicator. Because of this, the Navigator style may be frustrated by communication that does not get to the point or bottom-line. This is also the fundamental concept that sparks conflict for the Navigator. When others speak to a Navigator and do not get to the point, do not discuss results, and do not emphasize the bottom line, the Navigator may abruptly interrupt the conversation and request this information. The person at the other end of the conversation may become frustrated by the Navigator's abrupt, brief, and quick style. This lack of understanding and lack of adjustment widens the rift of differences. This rift plays a tremendous part in conflict.

Beyond differences in communication, what else may spark conflict for a Navigator type? Navigators may become agitated and even more authoritative when jobs are not completed on time, when the situation is highly "touchy-feely", when they lack (or feel as if they lack) control, when logic is lost, and when communication is not brief or to the point.

Many Navigator styles will handle these situations with an attitude that many others consider controlling or rude. Many Navigator styles are surprised at what others think of their actions. However, these Navigators are quick to mention that they don't care what others think of their management actions, and more importantly, they would not have acted in this manner if others would have done their job on time, or been more professional and brief in their communications. Playing the "he said, she said" game in business does not help to improve relations, results, or morale, yet the blame game is often played. This is the beginning of conflict.

> *I never give them hell; I just tell them the truth and they think it is hell* ~ Harry S. Truman

Social Servitor Style

The Social Servitor is typically a warm and friendly communicator. Because of this, the Social Servitor style may be frustrated by communication that does not attend to the ideas, needs, or input of other individuals. The Social Servitor prefers conversation that is more diplomatic and democratic in nature. When these elements are not included, the Social Servitor may nod his head, bite his tongue, and simmer until the frustration builds to a speedy boil. These facets are critical in creating conflict with the Social Servitor.

Recall this style typically does not manage personal conflict well, although they are excellent mediators for others in conflict. Because they may hide from personal conflict, they may not assert their ideas, needs, or frustrations. Instead, they bottle these issues within, perhaps venting to individuals who are not directly involved. When they tell someone of the issues, and that person tells someone else, and that person tells someone else, rumors begin. Rumors beget conflict.

Beyond these elements of communication, what else may spark conflict with the Social Servitor? One thing in particular that may seed conflict is when others ask Social Servitors to do favors for them, even if they know that person is swamped! The ironic thing (based on gentle nature and a lack of assertiveness) is that the Social Servitors more often will agree to do this task, and then become peeved that they were asked in the first place! Here is a prime example of the should've phenomenon... We think someone "should've" known about our other responsibilities. We think others "should've" known how we were feeling. We think people "should've" known this communication style does not work for us. Surprise! Most people are not telepathic, so it is important to be genuine, assertive, and diplomatic.

I believe in grumbling. It is the politest form of fighting known
~ Ed Howe

Explorer Style

The Explorer is typically an informal, spontaneous, colorful communicator. Because of this, the Explorer style may be frustrated by communication that does not have the flare of fun, spontaneity, or creativity. A lack of these concepts may be one of the greatest sources of conflict for the Explorer. When others speak to an Explorer in only terms of logic, deadlines, structure, or project, the Explorer may just tune out (intentionally or not). The mind of an Explorer seems to go a mile a minute, and when bored, the mind will quickly move to a thought or daydream that may entertain the Explorer. In this, the Explorer may not heed all of the information shared, may become frustrated when expected to respond to the topic missed, or may rebel when put on the spot for their inattention.

As we have discussed, the Explorer style may be prone to rebellion and stubborn streaks. Because of this, when someone tries to control the Explorer's "lack of attention", the Explorer type may rebel and make things more difficult than necessary. They do not like to be "forced to do" anything. They prefer to **do** because they want to **do**. This rebellious spirit can easily be taken the wrong way by those who do not understand or appreciate the Explorer's tremendous creativity and independence. This misunderstanding, again, easily leads to conflict.

What are some other activities that spark conflict with the Explorer? Well, simply, boredom! When an Explorer is bored, often he may consciously (or subconsciously) start an argument (heated discussion) just to change things up, to get something rolling, or to simply entertain. Most others do not see these discussions in such an innocent light and may turn them into a personal battle.

Other things that may provoke conflict with the Explorer type include micromanagement, attention to details, disrespect of their time, or doing tasks in order to justify someone else's position. As you can see, much of this may easily relate to the need for independence, for trust, for creative thought, and for some sense of freedom.

> *An oppressed people are authorized whenever they can to rise and break their fetters ~ Henry Clay*

Worker Style

The Worker is typically a formal, structured and detailed communicator. Because of this, the Worker style may be frustrated by communication that does not address specifics, that jumps quickly from topic to topic, or that does not have a sense of structure. A lack of these concepts may be one of the greatest sources of conflict for the Worker. When others speak to a Worker in only terms of fun, big picture, emotion, or personal issues, the Worker type may rebel in their own nature (leading to conflict). This rebellion includes withdrawal from the group meetings or working on projects while others are talking.

Much like the Social Servitor, the Worker is not fond of conflict and would rather avoid it than address it. However, there are times when the Worker style spurs conflict.

For instance, if they delegated tasks to others, and if those tasks were sloppily completed, the Worker style may become very agitated. The Worker may firmly (and with great tension) address the sloppy work of the individual. This attention to detail and need for work to be done correctly may be considered "anal" by others. These different views are ripe for misunderstanding and conflict.

What are some other aspects that spark conflict for a Worker style? A Worker may become greatly agitated and reduced to conflict when people interrupt their work in order to "chat", when others do not fulfill their role on the team, when they are asked to share their personal feelings or stories, when structure is shaken out of sheer boredom, or when people skip from topic to topic. They tend to think that these situations are a waste of time, prevent any real productivity, or disrespect their drive for accuracy and reliability.

From principles is derived probability, but truth or certainty is only derived from facts ~ Nathaniel Hawthorne

Dealing with Conflict

The best way to deal with conflict is to understand the behavioral and communication styles of all involved. Until we speak in the style that is most preferred by the other individual, we may not be able to effectively communicate or manage conflict. As leaders, stakeholders, or just interested individuals, it is critical to adjust styles to meet the needs or natural preferences of others. When this is done, those other individuals may attend more closely, may rebel less often, or may be more receptive and open to the task.

In addition to recognizing the preferred style of others, it is also important to attend to some basic conflict resolution steps.

1. Allow each party to speak uninterrupted. Ask that the discussions refrain from name calling or other judgmental terms. Expect that this discussion is to be attended and heard by all involved. Each party takes turns divulging their "side".

2. Be certain that every party is able to paraphrase the issue presented by the individual, with acknowledgment of accuracy by the speaker. In this, you are certain everyone has at least listened and accurately heard the message.

3. Allow each person to suggest what they think would be a fair solution. In addition, brainstorm for a win-win solution to all. Emphasize the need for win-win and not lose-lose or win-lose. Be certain everyone has had a chance to offer ideas, and that as many of those ideas from each person is implemented. People tend to support and complete those things which they created.

4. Complete a letter of agreement, outlining the nature of the proposed solution (who will do what, when and so on). Also, note what the consequences will be if this agreement is compromised or broken in any way. Be certain each party signs the document, even if it written on a paper napkin! Send a copy to each party.

Causing Problems at Work

Each of these behavioral styles can also cause problems at work if they are misunderstood, forced to conflict, or ignored. Recognizing some of the reasons behind the behavior is an important step in managing the undesired actions. Now, it is important to note that each individual is unique and we each have unique needs. With that said, it is evident that you will have to analyze a situation in order to truly understand the reason behind actions. We will discuss some problems you may find in the workplace to give you an idea of why people may act the way they do.

Have you ever wondered why some people thrive when personal drama surrounds them, or why some people seem to fail when they truly can excel, or why conflict seems to follow certain people? These are some of the problems we will discuss in this chapter.

Personal Drama

Some people thrive when they are involved with others. Many Social Servitors and Explorer styles thrive when in group settings or when given ample attention. It should not surprise you, then, to know that many times these styles will consciously or subconsciously create personal drama. Why? Often, this personal drama is coincidentally timed to periods when they may not be receiving much individual attention or group contact. In order to meet their needs of connection, personal drama "suddenly occurs." Sometimes, this is deliberate, and other times, the drama just seems to find them.

How can you manage this? Attend to their need to be of service to others, to be the center of some attention, and to give them the opportunity to show their creative side. This may mean giving them more time to express their stories, to brainstorm ideas, or to share their personal situations. While this sounds like torture to a Worker or Navigator, the time it takes to feed the sense of belonging is much less than the time it takes to clean up rumors, morale shifts, or sloppy work because of "personal drama." Again, we see that adaptation and adjustment, the sign of intelligence, is important in preventing or managing problems at work (or at home).

> *Make yourself necessary to somebody ~ Ralph Waldo Emerson*

Failing vs. Excelling

So, you have carefully chosen the members to your team. You have analyzed their strengths, weaknesses, and new role. You are confident you have assembled the best team, and that each member is well suited for their role.

Why has this team failed?

One of the common reasons that a team fails, even after extensive consideration and planning, is because you have a saboteur on board. Perhaps this person is sabotaging the project because they do not want to return to their other role. For instance, maybe that person is an Explorer and is on this team for his great trouble-shooting and creative ideas. His other role does not embrace these aspects. He is having more fun in this role!

Perhaps that person is sabotaging the project because they have a sense of belonging in the group that they may not feel in their other role (i.e. a Social Servitor). Perhaps that person is a saboteur because this project allows her to be in control and to flex her leadership muscle (the Navigator). Or perhaps the saboteur finds that everyone respects his time and attention to detail more so than those he works with in his other role (the Worker).

The best way to find out why people are intentionally, or unintentionally, sabotaging the project is to ask each individual what works for them. Why do they like this project? (do they? Maybe they just want to go back to their other task!) What do they look forward to, with this project or with a team that excelled? By asking what works or what could work instead of what is wrong, the emphasis is on solutions and not on the obstacle. With a temporary team, we want to move forward as quickly and as effectively as possible.

Other reasons why the team may fail instead of excel is fear. Fear of failure versus fear of success. To truly address this, again, we need to talk to each member individually and find out whether or not they want the project to succeed. Perhaps they are afraid that if they succeed, they may be transferred or promoted and they don't wish this to occur. Perhaps they are afraid that if the project is a success, others will raise the bar of expectation, and they may not be able to meet the newly raised bar (fear of failure). What would they love to have happen? What are they hoping does not happen? This is more analytical in nature and will take some time and attentive listening, but it is well worth the time.

> *Nothing in life is to be feared. It is only to be understood*
> *~ Madame Curie*

Conflict Follows

We talked about conflict and how to manage it. You still may be wondering why some people seem to be magnets to conflict. There are two common possibilities for this.

First, some people thrive off of the excitement that correlates with conflict and battle. Because of this rush, they may intentionally seek out conflict. Others find that conflict is a way to brainstorm ideas, find out what problems are truly present, and to progress! Either way, they seem open to conflict and the results it brings.

Second, some people actually see conflict as a means to compete. Competition is a strong drive for some individuals (many of whom are Navigators.) Without many opportunities to compete, these individuals will fill that void in some other way. Conflict seems to be a common substitute, although it is not necessarily as healthy as a good ole fashioned sprint to the finish line!

Handling these types of individuals who seem to be a magnet for conflict is not tricky. Feed the need. For instance, if they are competitive, give them a sense of competition, of winning, of team relations, and of glory in victory. If they are seeking the thrill of conflict, then brainstorm healthier ways to fulfill the need for excitement. The reason you want to brainstorm with them is because they are typically exceptionally creative beings who will follow-through on something much more often if they had a part in it from the beginning.

Myers' Problem Solving Model

Isabel Briggs Myers (one of the pair who developed the MBTI), also explored methods to solve problems that are based on personality differences. The model she developed continues to be dependable and reliable. In fact, many additional methods have been created using these four concepts as a base for their models.

Myer's model includes four factors and is actually simple and effective. The factors to solve problems include:

1. Get the facts. Explore the objective specific of the issue. Be certain to keep emotion at bay and clearly discuss the data. This is the phase at which Worker types excel.

2. Brainstorm the options (brainstorming is popular with problem solving!). Be creative; entertain all the options, no matter how crazy they sound at first. Let the ideas flow without restriction. Explorer types love this phase!

3. Objectively analyze each of the brainstormed options. Now is the time to think about the pros and cons, the how and why of each idea. It is looking at the big picture, as well as the possible results. The Navigator tends to take charge with this phase.

4. Explore the impacts that each of these options will have on others. How will they feel about this choice? Will they embrace it

or buck it? What will it do to the team morale? How is the intuition (or gut feeling) playing with the option? Social Servitors do well with this phase.

While some of the phases seem better suited for one style more than another phase might, it is important that all individuals (no matter what their preferred type) are involved in each phase in order to get the best results.

Conclusion

Wherever there are people, there will be problems. Without problems and conflict, our ancestors may not have felt the push to change and develop. Some problems may not be as noticeably positive in nature. With these, it is important to discover the reason behind them. More importantly, is the need to discover solutions to the issue at hand.

As mentioned, these are not the only problems you may find in the workforce, but they are common issues. Techniques to handle these issues are presented with hopes that you will be able to manage (or even prevent) these problems from impeding your project and team.

Social advance depends as much upon the process through which it is secured as upon the result itself ~ Jane Addams

Chapter Eight
FAQ's From Team Leaders & Project Managers

This chapter is dedicated to all those project managers and team leaders who offered questions that inspired this book. It will be written in a Q and A format, with the most commonly asked questions presented. These questions were sent to me from across the United States and Canada. There were many questions and challenges, and it was common that several questions were best represented by one submission. Therefore, I chose one submission to represent a group of common questions and challenges. I hope you find this chapter to be helpful and useful to you!

> *No man really becomes a fool until he stops asking questions*
> *~ Charles Steinmetz*

Lee: *"Why do folks have to be nagged to get their work done? In other words, what is or is not done for people to proactively take on issues and solve problems?"*

Answer: Unfortunately (or fortunately), not everyone emphasizes tasks or issues in the same manner. This issue can be addressed by shifting styles. For instance, it could very well be that the project manager has a preference for the Navigator style (focus on project, deadlines, results) and team members have a preference for one of the three other styles. Because of this, the team members do not place much emphasis on deadlines or results. The best way to positively move towards the end product is to coach them. Ask positive questions, use the terms of their preferred style. For instance, when talking with an individual who prefers the Social Servitor style, ask, "Where do you see improvements can be made to enhance the team's results? What contributions can you make from here on to help the project and morale of the team? What do you think the rewards or consequences should be if this is not accomplished?" This conversation could take 10 minutes or one hour, and follow-up, quick coaching connections can be scheduled as well.

Coaching, offering feedback and using their preferred style to hit the home run can help inspire others towards action and proactive solutions.

Renee: *"With most projects, the project manager is faced with leading and managing a virtual team. One in which all members play important roles and fill important criteria but in effect do not fall under the project manager's direct line of supervision. How does a PM effectively lead and monitor, as well as assertively manage a group that would consist of not only subordinates and peers but also supervisors (without resorting to being bossy, pushy, overbearing and similar adjectives)?"*

Answer: The topic of virtual teams continues to be of great interest, with meetings being held all over the globe via webinars, conference calls, or face to face meetings. How do we stay in contact, promote cohesion, and maintain independence? These issues are under great research.

This question asks: how can one effectively manage a group that is scattered throughout the company, managing subordinates, peers and supervisors? This can be tricky. Again, I may refer to style stepping, particularly when not wanting to be considered bossy, pushy or whatnot.

With various project teams, the connection can last a day, or a week, or a year! With the shorter termed teams, one may not be able to truly get to know one another, but recognizing their preferred style can help to ease the adjustment period.

I understand the importance of being able to quickly and accurate disseminate information regarding the project, especially when it is difficult to get the team together. What is important is for each member to feel as if they are an acting part of the group, as if they have some input in the process (meeting times, ideas, troubleshooting...). Knowing that a Worker type may be comfortable when given time to think about the options and come up with a solution instead of responding on the spot is one example of how to adjust with the team. Perhaps the Navigator and Explorer styles will offer ideas on the spot, but the Worker and even the Social Servitor styles prefer to think about the issues before responding. If this is the case, give them time to think and a deadline of response.

When giving information, cover all the bases and note that not everyone wants everything. For instance, provide detailed hand outs and say, "I realize not everyone needs all of the details, but for those who do, here they are!" In this, you are recognizing that the Workers thrive for this information (preferably in writing) and others may not want to sift through the specifics so readily.

Taking time to get to know each member, even if it is for only a few minutes at a time, can help the project manager get the information across with less effort or error.

Lester: *How can or what should a project manager do to effectively keep and help keep project members or stakeholders motivated to complete project deliverables timely and with quality?*

Answer: Motivation is a constant issue in the workplace and at home. If there were one magic pill or action that inspires motivation and action, our world would be so different! But, as we all know from experience, there does not seem to be that magical one-size-fit-all solution. So, how can we encourage this motivation to complete tasks with quality and style?

In my book, *Motivation and Inspiration*, I discuss the most common factors with motivation. Fear may work at some point with a few folks, but it is not something to rely on for a great, consistent effect. Communication is a huge factor in motivation. When people understand one another, they tend to work hard for each other. Trust and loyalty have a huge impact on whether or not things are accomplished, and accomplished with quality. To gain trust and loyalty, we need to embrace the strengths of others and be certain to recognize (and somehow fulfill) their needs as well. So much to do!

As you can see, software and the technical side of things may not have a tremendous, universal motivational impact on many people. The focus here is people.

One of the best questions to ask your team members is: "What are two or three realistic things that would motivate you towards quality, on-time project deliverables?" I suggest people ask this question near the beginning of their team development, perhaps after a hands-on, team activity. Write down their answers. Use those things, even if YOU would not be motivated by them! We each have different needs and different preferred styles of communication. Taking the extra effort and time to personalize feedback or praise can be a strong motivator.

Kim: *"If I could ask one question, it would be "what are you most afraid of"? Project team members will tailor their communications based on anticipated reactions or consequences. The PM needs to be aware of what each person's "filter" is, and how strong it is. Fear of communicating, especially anything that negatively impacts a project, can substantially hurt the project."*

Answer: Kim is right on the nose with this observation. Some people, more notable those who prefer the Social Servitor or Worker styles, tend to say nothing or tailor their response in order to prevent any sort of conflict. With this, their responses may not be completely honest, and their dedication to the task may waiver.

Think of your team members and write down what you consider to be their preferred communication styles. Talk to them in their style and you may have greater opportunities to get honest feedback from them. By privately visiting with the Worker style, and allowing them time to process the information, you may get some very insightful and creative responses. By reassuring the Social Servitor that their ideas are appreciated, will be considered, and will not be cause for conflict, you may receive honest and deeply-thought responses. With those who prefer the Navigator or Explorer styles, they do not fear conflict and will readily speak their mind. However, they do have fears that may taint their responses. For instance, the Navigator does not want to lose a sense of control and will tailor their actions so they can maintain that feeling of control and leadership. Along the same lines, the Explorer may fear losing their sense of independence and freedom. Therefore, they may tailor responses to assure these qualities remain. By assuring your team that these needs or qualities will not be affected by their ideas, you may find the brainstorming and troubleshooting sessions to be extremely energetic and creative.

Julinda: As a team leader and project manager, how do I keep all the team members feeling informed and engaged, especially when the time pressures of multiple projects are put on the team? The first thing that suffers is the communications (attending status meetings, reading update emails, etc).

Answer: Many project managers can attest to their team being spread too thin, although they do note that many of those projects are completed on-time and with expected quality. The best answer for this would be, "just expand your resources... hire more folks to help with the projects." Is this realistic? Not even close. So, what is the realistic solution? Some team members prefer the email approach, others prefer the phone approach, and others seek a face to face meeting. All of this takes time, and time is not always forgiving.

Managing the use of time is crucial. It is important to have team meetings, even if just for a few moments every day or once per week. Note that some people may prefer the details to be conveyed in writing so they can think these over. Allow this to occur, even if it means assigning someone to take minutes and send it out to each member. Others may desire more personal means of connection. Scheduling time to allow this, even if brief and occasional, will encourage the team members to feel more included and involved. With this sense of inclusion and involvement comes the greater sense of responsibility and accountability, which can then improve productivity and quality.

So, think of it in this manner: You are working on four tasks. One of those tasks involves working with a manager who takes an extra five minutes to connect with you, in a way you like. The other three managers don't talk to you the way you like, and you often leave with unanswered questions because of this. To whom would you naturally want to give more time? The old adage holds true in this situation as well, "you attract more flies with honey than with vinegar".

By investing time (which is short, I know!) and meeting the preferred communication style of your team members, you will be able to keep everyone involved and accountable, while enhancing the morale of the team as a whole.

Walter: *I have been promoted and am now managing a group that includes people who were originally my peers before my promotion. How can I, and others in my situation, lead with a greater sense of confidence?*

Answer: Believe it or not, this is not a rare occurrence. No matter what the field, many people are promoted and then have to lead their cohorts. Sometimes, this is not always as smooth a transition as we hoped it would be.

Leading with confidence includes feeling confident in your abilities. There are reasons why people are promoted, and we hope that their abilities have some impact on that decision of promotion! Taking a step back to see the abilities others see in you is important in smooth transitions.

Furthermore, meet with the team and openly explore your expectations of them and their expectations of you. Doing so can help a newly appointed leader start the position with clear guidelines and appreciation from the team for their interest and input.

In addition, as you may have guessed, truly connecting with each member and addressing each member in the preferred style can further enhance the loyalties, trust, and leadership among each member of the team. This can improve relations and production, which can build the confidence of team members for their leader.

Don: *How do you convey a consistent sense of responsibility or urgency in delivering quality end of month deliverables to the prime contractor?*

Answer: What one person may consider urgent, another person may not consider urgent. How can we get people on the same page?

Often, a task is due on a particular date. Ok, fine. Here is the problem: some people may not think the task is important. So they procrastinate, doing the things they LIKE first (again, see the different behavioral styles). What I have seen work in the past is to inform folks (using the language that best suits them: using their preferred style) of the reason behind the task and deadline. How does this affect others? (Social Servitors may really connect to this). How can this task be done well (right) AND on time? (Worker types will connect to this). How can meeting this deadline help in maintaining independence (or how can missing it impede freedom? Explorer styles will connect to this). What is the big picture and how does the deliverable play a part in it? (Navigator styles will relate to this).

In addition, when you meet with each of these contracting parties, it is important to ask them how they would like to be contacted, what they expect of you and of themselves, and what consequences they prefer for you and themselves if the project is not done as expected. Getting the information up front with the project charter (and with subtle reminders throughout the month) attracts accountability and responsibility and this enhances results.

Beth: *Team members buy into the project charter, but then later other multiple outside influences or other projects (for which you are not responsible) come into play, and the team member is no longer as interested in the project that you are managing.*

How can you minimize the effects of these influences?

Answer: Keeping your project at the top of everyone's list is important. This can be somewhat difficult when new projects come into play. Take, for instance, the Explorer style. This style typically bores easily when situations lag (like when projects are no longer "new and exciting"). Keeping your project of interest to them requires keeping them in the project loop. People who feel as if the project is THEIR project do not tend to leave it hanging. However, those who feel as if they are just one more individual working on the task may easily let your project go.

How do you build buy-in and accountability? Connecting with your team members on a consistent basis can improve chances to keep your project on the top. In this connection, be certain to step into their style and emphasize the things they are most interested in. Get their input and heed their ideas in accordance to their preferred communication style. Using their style is comfortable for them, and this affords them more availability for your project.

One simple thing to do in the beginning of the project is to inform your members, "I know in a month or more, you will be working on several projects. This project is as much yours as it is mine. What are some ways you would like to be kept an important part of the project? What are some ways we can keep this project at the top of your list, even when you have a number of other deliverables?" Use these ideas. This means writing them down and remembering them!

Saiful: *Communication is one of the major factors that caused people-oriented problem in my organization. Different perceptions, understanding, and personalities force people to see things differently. I find it hard some times to communicate the importance of a task to subordinates. Some people cannot see the big picture or lack the ability to visualize things from broader term. Is there an easy means to communicate the big picture and connectivity to subordinates?*

Answer: While there may not be an easy means to emphasize the big picture and connectivity to others, stepping into their style to communicate these aspects can help. Some people naturally do not see the big picture and need some additional guidance to do so. For instance, when communicating with one who prefers the Worker style, the natural emphasis for them is the detail of the project. By building on the detail and structurally exploring how those details effect (and are effected by) the big picture, the Worker may be able to better see the big picture.

Connecting various levels of the project is also important. Because of this, emphasis should be on the style of communication as much as it should be on the message. When really studying the message but ignoring the way the message is sent, we leave a tremendous amount of room for misunderstanding or misinterpretation. By attending to both the style of communication as well as to the message, it may be much easier for the listener to connect the importance of their task when it comes to the deliverable and the deadlines.

Annette: *The problem is that our management has not been trained in project management and does not always understand our challenges. As a result, we are short-staffed on most of our projects, even though we've requested them to be fully staffed. Attempts to show the issues with this are usually "illogically" refuted. I feel that sometimes control is the issue in our organization as we move from a functional type environment to a more project-oriented environment. How can we, as project managers, resolve these types of conflicts metrically and peacefully?*

AND:

Craig: *My biggest challenge is matrix management as it relates to getting functional managers to appropriately staff up for the IT projects without which, too much time is spent negotiating for resources, posting or interviewing resources, and securing resources from being sniped by another (i.e. higher priority) project.*

AND:

Pam: *How do you deal with acquisition of resources when everyone always has a "full plate" and you get only partial attention to your project because it isn't the highest priority in the organization?*

Answer: Annette, Craig, Pam and others have asked this very question regarding resources and the project management vs. traditionally corporate environment. Being a psychologist, I can field this question from the psychological point of view. The biggest way to expand resources, resolve conflicts, or gain support is to show people how the project or department will benefit them. Again, the best way to do this is to emphasize the areas most important to that person.

For instance, a Navigator type may want to know the big picture, bottom line, results, and how it will be of benefit to that person or the company as a whole. How will the Navigator excel by the project management team? What is in it for him or her?

The Worker type will want to see the numbers, the research, and the benefits of additional resources within project management. They may even want to see specific benefits from other companies who doubted the benefits from investing with a project management environment. With both the Navigator and Worker styles, your message will get across better by using terms dealing with logic (think, analyze, numbers...)

When dealing with Social Servitors, your focus will be vastly different than it will be when you are talking to Navigator or Worker styles. The Social Servitor will want to know how the additional resources will impact the budget (which impacts personnel). They may want to know what type of training this will involve. More likely, they will lean to a democratic decision, seeking the opinions and approval of others. If you can show how people are positively impacted, and how other companies have succeeded (personally and corporately), you may be gaining greater interest. In addition, seek the opinion of others and then visit with the Social Servitor to gain their attention. You may have their attention much more quickly than if you have no idea what their colleagues think of the idea of expanding the project management department.

Finally, when discussing issues like this with the Explorer style, express how quickly things can move, how innovative the environment can be, how the resources can impact his or her independence and freedom, and how this can enhance the creative flow of the department. They may still be interested in the bottom line and the results, but they want to know how it can be accomplished without micromanagement and without additional work or supervision on their part.

Hopefully, by specifying different aspects of the project management request, you will be able to truly connect with each of these leaders on a level they find comfortable and in a way that is win-win for all.

Rebecca: *How can I motivate my project resources to keep me (their project manager) informed of their issues, progress, and problems (in place of, or in addition to, their supervisor)?"*

Answer: Think of a time when you had to talk business with someone you respect, like, or know. Compare that to a time when you had to talk business with someone you don't respect, don't like, or don't know. Who would you rather talk to? For the purposes of this question, the idea is very similar. People will talk to people who listen to, respect, and know them.

So, to keep communication open, it is important to develop a strong base of respect, trust, and interest. This way, when there is a problem, team members are not worried about how badly they will be chewed out, but are concerned with collectively coming to a quick and effective solution.

Explain to your team that you respect their ideas; model to them that fear is not a motivator you choose to use, and use positive coaching techniques. These actions will encourage continuous communication, not matter what the situation.

Furthermore, to gain loyalty and trust, take time to address issues that are important to them. For a Social Servitor, this may include the family issues going on at home. For the Explorer, it may include the desire to become more autonomous on the job. Using these issues will build a sense of genuine interest in them. When people sense that you are genuinely interested in their job or in them as a person, they are more apt to be interested in you. Having the mutual respect and interest truly helps when people need to feel comfortable enough to discuss problems and brainstorm solutions.

Another technique to use is to ask your members what has worked for them in the past when they felt comfortable enough to talk to their manager about problems or progress. If possible, use these ideas. Also ask them what works for them as a means for them to receive information about the project's progress or issues. In this, they feel important to be kept abreast of the issues (if they want to), and they have a great sense of buy-in and accountability.

Luis: What are the most common reasons for people-oriented problems within projects and what can I do as a PM to avoid or mitigate those problems.

Answer: This is a great question, Luis, and I wish I had an easy answer for you. From all of the feedback I have had on this survey, my understanding is that the biggest people-oriented problems stem from miscommunication and conflict. For those who wished to comment further, it appears that miscommunication and conflict occur because people do not understand one another. This has everything to do with various communication, behavioral, and yes, personality styles. Those responses (and very specific questions just like yours) are what spurred this book, so I hope you find a wealth of information on how to prevent or manage miscommunication and conflict based on behavioral and communication differences.

> *I am prejudiced in favor of him, who, without impudence, can ask boldly. He has faith in humanity, and faith in himself. No one who is not accustomed to giving grandly can ask nobly and with boldness ~ Johann Kaspar Lavater*

Conclusion

Many project managers and team leaders tell of times when people problems devastated projects. They tell of the conflict their teams experience because they just "can't get along". The tone seems to be one of frustration because their team members were able to carry out their job, but when grouped together, the ability seemed to vanish next to the differences in communication, behavior, and personal preferences. Do these projects have to be this way? Hopefully, after reading this book or experiencing a Social Compass interpersonal effectiveness training, you have come to the decision that no, projects and teams do not have to be ineffective.

Is it easy to change the function of one's projects or teams? Well, it is not difficult, but it does take practice and conscious effort to work. What is difficult is to actually work the projects and teams in the same manner, dealing with constant interpersonal issues, misunderstandings, and different preferences in action. So, as the saying goes, if you continue to do what you have always done, you will continue to get the results you have always gotten.

> *There are two ways of meeting difficulties: you alter the difficulties or you alter yourself meeting them ~ Phyllis Bottome*

Along this thought, it is important to be conscientious in recognizing the various personal preferences of others, in adjusting styles when communicating with others, in coaching team members for improved performance or professional development, and in providing and eliciting feedback for desired results.

Know your objective. Look at your Social Compass for the most effective heading to achieve that objective. Adjust your style to suit the situation, individual, and results.

One of my favorite sayings is: Mindful behavior beats mindless behavior. This is not only true when thinking of how we send a message, but also is true when dealing with any type of action (like reacting to brash customers, to overeating, or to driving in rush hour...) You will find the more you can deliberately act or react, the better the results. For some of us, this deliberate, mindful behavior may be easier to hone, and for others, it may take more discipline. No matter what the comfort, it is important to rehearse these concepts so that mindful communication (adjusting styles) is habit.

Habits take about six weeks to form (except for those relating to addictive substances). No matter what you are trying to improve, give yourself six weeks of conscious effort to develop the habit. This works for adjusting your communication style, for establishing an exercise regime, for developing a healthy diet, and many other behaviors. Here are some important keys to establishing good habits:

1. Be mindful and conscientious when establishing habits. As time progresses, habits become stronger and require less thought to continue working.

2. Reward yourself when you are mindful in establishing habits. People do not

celebrate nearly enough. If we continue working hard towards a greater goal but do not reward the smaller accomplishments needed to reach the bigger goal, we are more apt to become frustrated or to give up when an obstacle arises. Rewards can help with motivating us. The rewards do not have to be big, but they do need to be effective. They need to follow the behavior or to be a conscious reward for the action achieved.

3. When practicing habits, like adjusting styles, it is very effective when you can see or hear what it is you are doing or saying. In this, use a camcorder or audio-recorder to record your rehearsal. Do you have to rehearse with another person? It helps, but I have had clients tell me they rehearse to themselves, using people they know as models for how the other imaginative person responds.

4. When you have established your habit, don't just let it go. It takes less effort to maintain a habit than it did to establish a habit, so continue to rehearse and be mindful of improving that behavior. Whatever you do, reward yourself when you have reached your goal!

Research

If you have experienced the Social Compass training, you have joined more than 50 million people who have experienced interpersonal effectiveness training! The vast majority of people have noted that the four dimensions within personality or temperament are an easy and accurate guideline to follow when working with others. Not only that, but the number of people who experience training like this is skyrocketing. This statistic reveals the importance and effectiveness of interpersonal training like the Social Compass, MBTI, DiSC, True Colors, PeopleMap and others.

Many of these profiles and trainings also emphasize the importance of reliability and validity. Reliability is the ability to be consistent in the measurement. This is also the ability to generalize to the greater community, and still be accurate. Validity is the ability to measure what it is intended to measure. Think of a bathroom scale. What is it intended to measure? Weight! If it did not accurately measure weight, it would not be valid, since it was designed to measure weight. These are important with the Social Compass, MBTI, DiSC and others.

Research in project management supports what I have heard from project managers across the country: People-oriented issues have a big impact on the quality and effectiveness of projects. Project managers note the importance of interpersonal effectiveness training, and many emphasize the desire to train everyone in their team! Of course, resources are already slim, so this may not be feasible. However, even if the project managers and team leaders can share the basic information to team members, they may be able to see positive results when it comes to team interaction and project effectiveness.

The concepts behind the Social Compass stem back to Hippocrates. He thought that temperaments can be divided into one of four groups: Sanguine, Choleric, Phlegmatic, or Melancholic. From there, many philosophers and scientists studied personalities and behaviors and continue to support the idea that people's personalities, behavioral, or communication preferences can be divided into four central themes.

Predecessors to the Social Compass who have conducted extensive studies in the field of personality and behavioral methods include Isabel Myers (of the MBTI and who based her research on Carl Jung's principals), David Keirsey (who refined the work of Isabel Myers and the MBTI and developed the Keirsey Temperament Sorter) and William Moulton Marston (who developed the principles found in the DiSC profile).

The Social Compass is founded on the same principles. Furthermore, the Social Compass has a solid foundation on emotional intelligence and positive psychology. In this, it is important to play upon strengths and build those areas that can become strengths. We recognize that people are dynamic, and it is important to be able to adjust in order to match the issue at hand. Being interpersonally effective also leads to being an advanced and competent leader.

This book, training, and profile are not meant as a means to assess mental illness. This profile and training addresses issues that may develop with people of sound mind. You may be working with someone dealing with narcissistic tendencies, with paranoid personality disorders, or any number of issues. This book does not address these issues, nor should it be used as a mental health guideline for people suffering from mental illness. In this case, it is important to see a clinical psychologist, psychiatrist, counseling therapist, or mental health facility for treatment or direction.

About Dr. Dawdy

Reach Peak Potential with Peak Strategies: An organizational training, executive coaching, leadership development firm.

Gwynne N. Dawdy is an Organizational Psychologist and a National Certified Counselor. She is an experienced consultant in the fields of leadership development, personality and social styles, team management, conflict resolution, communication, sport psychology, and health wellness.

She has a Ph.D. in industrial/organizational psychology; a MS specialized in sport psychology, and a MA in counseling and psychology. She is a trainer, consultant, executive coach and author.

Dr. Dawdy's professional experiences include training, coaching, and consulting in the fields of performance enhancement, accelerated project/team management skills, leadership, group cohesion, communication, relationships, goal getting, motivation, and stress management.

Training Topics and Services:

Social Styles and Behavioral Preferences
Communication Styles
Leadership Development
Coaching in the Workplace
Team Cohesion
Motivation
Conflict Resolution

Goal Achievement
Sport Psychology and Performance
Enhancement

We specialize in ½ or full day workshops, teleseminars, and executive coaching for project managers, team leaders, and high potential personnel. These trainings are often conducted on-site or as open-enrollment courses for project management chapters, corporations, and other organizations. Many of our participants are leaders, project managers, human resource personnel, and educators who strive for greater success with less human effort.

Being able to live and use one's talents and potential to the fullest is optimal in many areas of life. In order to do this, one must be able to recognize the mental pitfalls and prevent them from engulfing one's energies and thoughts.

Some of these mental pitfalls include:
Interpersonal relation issues
Ineffective communication
Motivational issues
Unclear goals
Low confidence
Fear of failure or of success
Stress
Health issues

Dr. Dawdy's seminars and consultations are designed to troubleshoot these issues. Clients will learn to strengthen various aspects that effect work performance. This will help increase performance, confidence, management skills, and even physical and mental wellness and health.

With these strategies, people can enhance their productivity and their personal connections.

Contact Peak Strategies for more information, or to view or purchase additional products:

http://peakstrategies.net
ps@peakstrategies.net

P.O. Box 7034
Woodland Park, CO 80863

Printed in the United States
58264LVS00003B/172-471